# The Etiquette and Interpretation of Dreams

## Ahmed Farid

### Translated By
### Omar Kasir

This work has been selected by scholars as culturally important. The book has remained out of print and circulation for a long time; therefore, it has been reproduced from the original artifact and remains as true to the original work as possible. You will see the original copyright references, library stamps, and other notations in the work. As a reproduction of an artifact, this work may contain missing or blurred pages, poor pictures, errant marks, etc. Scholars believe, and we concur, that this work is important enough to be preserved, reproduced, and made generally available to the public. We appreciate the support of the preservation process and thank you for being an important part of keeping this knowledge alive and relevant

# Table of Contents

Preface..................................................................8
The Meaning and Types of Dreams.........................13
The Benefit of a Good Dream..................................19
   The Benefit of seeing the Prophet ﷺ in a Dream.......22
Etiquette of Seeing a Dream....................................27
   A - The Etiquette that a Muslim should adhere to so that his or her dream may come true........................27
      1. One must always tell the truth,......................27
      2 - A person should fear Allah ﷻ in all his affairs 29
      3 - Muslims should respect the etiquette of sleep. 30
      4 - One should ask Allah ﷻ to grant him a good dream..............................................................33
   B - The Etiquette that a person should adhere to after having a dream....................................................34
   C- The Etiquettes that interpreters of dreams should adhere to..............................................................40
Categories of Interpreting Dreams............................44
   A- Interpreting Dreams from a Qur'anic Perspective 44
      A Ship.............................................................44
      Wood..............................................................45
      Stones............................................................45
      Disease..........................................................45
      Eggs...............................................................45
      Water..............................................................46
      Meat................................................................46
      The Entry of a King........................................46
      Ascension to the Sky.....................................47
      Adhan.............................................................48
      Ruku...............................................................48
      Sujud..............................................................48
      Praying with the wrong Qiblah........................48
      The Ka'bah....................................................49

| | |
|---|---|
| Entering Makkah | 49 |
| Offering a Sacrifice | 50 |
| The Day of Judgement | 50 |
| Entering the Paradise | 51 |
| Entering the Hellfire | 51 |
| Cows | 51 |
| Parents | 52 |
| Allah's Anger | 52 |
| Salaah | 53 |
| A Dead Person | 53 |
| Hellfire | 53 |
| Old Age | 54 |
| Perfume | 54 |
| Play | 54 |
| A Shirt | 55 |
| Death | 55 |
| Entering a Door | 55 |
| A Bird Flying Overhead | 56 |
| Speaking to a Leader | 56 |
| An Army | 56 |
| Peace | 57 |
| Being Bound | 57 |
| Headache | 57 |
| A Bed | 58 |
| Being in a Room | 58 |
| Al-Qisas (Law of Equality) | 58 |
| Drinking Alcohol | 58 |
| The Waves of the Sea | 59 |
| Couches | 59 |
| Divorce | 60 |
| Treating a Person Unjustly | 60 |
| White Eyes | 60 |
| Blindness | 61 |
| Biting the Fingers | 61 |

| | |
|---|---|
| Sleep | 61 |
| A Pledge | 62 |
| The Sky | 62 |
| A Camel Entering | 62 |
| A Gift | 63 |
| Booty of War | 63 |

**B- Interpreting Dreams from the Perspective of the Hadith of Prophet Muhammad ﷺ** .......... 63

| | |
|---|---|
| A Crow or a Mouse | 63 |
| Ribs | 64 |
| Glass Vessels | 64 |
| Milk | 65 |
| Shirts | 66 |
| Fettered Feet | 67 |
| Water | 68 |
| Keys | 71 |
| A Palace | 72 |
| Wudu (Ablution) | 73 |
| Tawaf around the Ka'bah | 73 |
| A Sword | 74 |
| Cows | 75 |
| Blowing | 76 |
| Gold | 77 |
| Marriage | 78 |
| Silky Clothes | 79 |
| Clouds | 79 |
| A Green Garden | 82 |
| Scales | 83 |

**C- Interpreting Dreams from the Meaning of Names** 85

| | |
|---|---|
| A Knot | 86 |
| A Voice | 87 |
| Marriage, Eyesight, Peace and Charity | 87 |
| Remembrance of Allah and Gold | 87 |
| Europeans | 88 |

- Christians.................................................................88
- Jews..........................................................................88
- Beds..........................................................................88
- Sheep........................................................................89
- The Head...................................................................89
- Teeth.........................................................................89
- Surat Al-Fatihah ........................................................90
- A Key.........................................................................90
- A Necklace................................................................90
- Becoming a Monk.....................................................91
- Names........................................................................91

D. Interpreting Dreams from the Meaning of the Proverb......................................................................92
- A Long Hand..............................................................92
- Washing Hands..........................................................93
- A Pair of Scissors......................................................93

E. Interpreting Dreams by their Meaning....................93
- A Citrus Fruit............................................................93
- Flowers......................................................................94

F. Interpreting Dreams by their Opposite Meaning...94

Rules and Benefits Concering Dreams ............................96
Some Rare Interpretations of our Ancestors...................101
Glossary..............................................................................107

# Preface

All praise is due to Allah. We praise Him, seek His Aid and ask for His Forgiveness. We seek Allah's Refuge from the evils of ourselves and from the evil of our actions. Whomsoever Allah guides none can lead astray, and whomsoever Allah leads astray none can guide. I testify that none has the right to be worshipped but Allah ﷻ Alone, without partners, and I testify that Muhammad ﷺ is His Slave and Messenger.

Allah ﷻ says,
❮O ye who believe! fear Allah as He should be feared and die not, except in a state of Islam❯[1]

❮O mankind! Be careful of your duty to your Lord Who created you from a single soul, and from it created its mate and from them twain had spread abroad a multitude of men and women. Be careful of your duty toward Allah, in Whom you claim (your rights) of one another, and toward the wombs (that bore you). Lo! Allah had been a Watcher over you❯[2]

❮O you who believe! Fear Allah, and (always) say a good word: That He may make your conduct whole and sound and forgive you your sins: he that obeys

---

[1] Al-Imran: Verse 102.
[2] An-Nisa': Verse 1.

Allah and His Apostle has already attained the highest Achievement⟩³

The best speech is that embodied in the Book of Allah ﷻ, and the best guidance is the guidance given by Muhammad ﷺ. The most evil affairs are their innovations; and every innovation is a *Bid'ah* and every *Bid'ah* is a misguidance, and any misguidance is in Hellfire.

The interpretation of dreams is one of the greatest, comprehensive and most useful types of knowledge. The Prophet ﷺ said: "A good dream (that comes true) of a righteous man is one forty-sixth part of prophethood," and he ﷺ also said: "Nothing is left of the prophethood except *Al-Mubashshirat*." They asked, "What are *Al-Mubashshirat*?" He ﷺ replied, "The good true dreams (that convey glad tidings)."

Imam Malik ؓ was asked: "Can anyone interpret dreams?" He answered: "Can anyone play with prophethood." The Prophet ﷺ has forbidden us to ask anyone about the interpretation of dreams, except a scholar.

Due to the nobility and importance of this knowledge, Allah ﷻ has associated it with His Prophets and righteous servants. The two imprisoned men told Yusuf ؑ, ⟨ **inform us of the interpretation of this. Verily, we**

---
³ Al-Ahzaab: Verse 70-71.

think you are one of the *Mohsinun* (doers of good)❭⁴. The two men knew that only righteous people could interpret dreams. Likewise, Allah ﷻ had honoured Yusuf ﷺ by teaching him this noble knowledge (i.e. interpretation of dreams), as his father Ya'qub ﷺ said, when Yusuf ﷺ informed him of his dream, ❬thus will your Lord choose you and teach you the interpretation of dreams❭ ⁵

Yusuf ﷺ praised Allah ﷻ and increased His Favours and Benefits upon him, ❬My Lord! You have indeed bestowed on me of the sovereignty, and taught me the interpretation of dreams❭ ⁶

The importance of this knowledge is manifested clearly when someone has a bad dream and becomes confused, holding his breath as violent fear seizes him; yet, these bad dreams can turn into something good for him, and defeat his enemy. On the other hand, he might see a beautiful dream, and feel satisfied with it, yet it turns out to be his downfall and disappointment. No one can interpret either of the above dreams, and their meaning, except someone with this precious knowledge.

In an era when the banner of Sunnah is raised, Muslims are waiting for a new dawn, and since the demand for books on he interpretation of dreams is on the increase, I

---

⁴ Yusuf: Verse 36.
⁵ Ibid: Verse 6.
⁶ Ibid: Verse 101.

have decided to compile a book about the Etiquette and Interpretation of Dreams. I hope that Muslims, all over the world, would benefit from it and I ask Allah ﷻ for His Reward, on the Day of Judgement.

I do not claim that I have excelled in this knowledge, nor become an interpreter of dreams, but I am entirely dependent upon the works of the *Salaf Saleh* (righteous predecessors) and I only pass on their knowledge to the Muslims Ummah.

I have started my book with the meaning of dreams and their types. Then I have mentioned the benefit of a good dream, including the benefit of seeing the Prophet ﷺ in a dream. I have also mentioned the etiquettes of dreams, which includes etiquettes that a Muslim should comply with, so that his dreams could come true; etiquettes that a dreamer should adopt, and etiquettes of the interpreter.

Finally, I have mentioned the purpose of this book, that is, the interpretation of dreams according to the Qur'an, Sunnah Sahihah and the meaning of words, names, proverbs, etc.

People get confused when dealing with the issue of dreams; believing that a good dream could even be a source of legislation in Islamic Shari'ah. Therefore, they may use dreams to confirm Islamic rules, and even rely on them to determine whether Ahadeeth of the Prophet ﷺ are *Sahih* (authentic) or *Da'eef* (weak). Sufi sects have also exploited dreams enormously, in this manner. Accordingly, I have completed my book with a chapter about the rules of dreams and some rare stories from the Salafi interpreters of dreams, such as Ibn Sireen.

# The Meaning and Types of Dreams

Al-Hafidh Ibn Hajar, may Allah have Mercy upon him, said: "Al-Qadi Abu Bakr Ibn al-Arabi has said: "Dreams are perceptions placed in the heart of a person, in the hands of an angel or a devil, either in the form of names, (true nature), or surnames, (interpretation), or confusion. They are equivalent to thoughts and ideas in wakefulness, because they may come in a regular order, in the form of a story, or naturally." However, Abu Ishaaq has said: "Al-Qadi Abu Bakr Ibn at-Tayyib thinks that dreams are beliefs. He justified his argument by saying that a dreamer may see himself as an animal or a bird, for example, which is not perception; therefore, it must be a belief, as it may be unlike the thing perceived."[7]

However, the reader should know that not all the things that a dreamer sees in his sleep could have a meaning for interpretation. The dreamer may see one of the following three things:

**1- Confused, false dreams from Satan**, as in the story of the man who said to the Prophet ﷺ: "I saw in a dream that I had been beheaded, then I followed it (the severed head) and put it back in its place." Allah's Messenger ﷺ

---

[7] *Fa'th al-Bari*, (12/352,353).

said: "Do not talk about Satan's vain sporting with you, during the night."⁸ This is just one of Satan's vain ways of sporting; an artifice that may bring grief to the believers, which Allah ﷻ has informed us of in the Qur'an, **❲Secret counsels (conspiracies) are only from Satan, in order that he may cause grief to the believers❳** ⁹ Also, Satan may cause one to have a sexual dream, which requires one to take a bath. However, this requires no interpretation, and the Prophets were exempt of it, since the Prophets' dreams were revelations.

**2-** *Hadith an-Nafs***:** The reflection of one's thoughts and experiences one has when one is awake. For example, one might have been very busy with his business or voyage; then during his sleep he sees what he has been thinking about. These are also considered as confused dreams, although they are not from Satan, because they do not cause grief in the heart. In short, they are not true dreams, that entail glad tidings or warning, nor Satan's deceptions and insinuations, that bring about grief and pain.

**3- A Good Dream:** is from Allah ﷻ. For the believer, it is one forty-sixth part of prophethood. There is no doubt that part of a good dream is seeing the Prophet ﷺ. On the authority of Jabir ﷺ, the Prophet ﷺ said: "He who saw me in a dream, has, in fact, seen me, for Satan cannot

---

⁸ Sahih Muslim: 15/27, Ibn Majah: 3912 and al-Baghawi: *"Sharh as-Sunnah"*, 12/212.
⁹ Al-Mujadilah: Verse 10.

assume my form."[10] Satan cannot assume the form or natural disposition of the Prophet.☙

These three types of dreams may be summarized in a Hadith, reported by Abu Hurairah ☙, in which the Prophet ☙ said: "When the Day of Resurrection approaches, the dreams of a believer will hardly fail to come true, and a dream of a believer is one forty-sixth part of prophethood; and whatever belongs to prophethood can never be false. There are three types of dreams: A good dream which is a glad tiding from Allah, a dream suggested by Satan to frighten the dreamer, and a dream which is a reflection of the thoughts and experiences that one had while awake."[11]

One may ask oneself: how one could distinguish between these three types of dreams, and how one could know whether it was a good dream from Allah ☙, from Satan, or just self-reflection (*Hadith an-Nafs*)?

The answer is found by factual evidence of the dreamer himself, the nature of the dream, the time of the dream and the circumstances of the dream. If the dreamer is a sincere believer, most of the time his/her dreams should be glad tidings from Allah ☙. However, if the dreamer is a disbeliever or a sinner, most of what they see would be confused, false dreams. Sometimes disbelievers and

[10] Sahih Muslim: 15/26 and Ibn Majah: Hadith 3902.
[11] Sahih al-Bukhari: 12/404, Sahih Muslim: 15/20-21, Abu Dawud: 4998, at-Tirmidhi: 9/133, and al-Baghawi in his book "*Sharh as-Sunnah*": 12/208.

sinners see a true dream, but only as a warning, as in the story of the King in Surat Yusuf ﷺ.

The Prophets and Messengers were the most sincere believers and most upright in their words and deeds. Everything that they saw in their dreams was true, as Ibrahim ﷺ said to his son, ❰**I have seen in a dream that I was slaughtering you (offered you as a sacrifice to Allah), so what do you think? He said: 'O my father! Do that which you are commanded.'**❱ [12]

As for a *Hadith an-Nafs*, it comes to both believers and sinners, since it is neither from Allah ﷻ, nor from Satan with his insinuation and intimidation.

As for the good dreams they come in the form of clear signs and there is no confusion in them; the dreamer would remember them as if they were real. They are glad tidings for the believer to strengthen his hope in Allah ﷻ, as Allah says, ❰**those who believe and keep their duty to Allah, for them are glad tidings in the life of the present world and in the Hereafter**❱ [13] The Prophet ﷺ said: "A good dream is one which a believer sees or is shown;"[14] or a warning from an enemy, such as danger that a believer should prepare against. Therefore, a good dream from Allah ﷻ is accompanied by delight, joy and

---

[12] As-Safaat: Verse 102.
[13] Yunus: Verses 63-64.
[14] Reported by at-Tirmidhi: 9/127-128, who classified it as Hadith Hassan, Ibn Majah: 3898, Imam Malik in "*Al-Muwatta*'": 2/958, al-Hakim: 4/391.

an increase of faith; the believer feels that it is a Blessing and Mercy from Allah ﷻ.

As for a dream that is part of Satan's insinuations, it comes in the form of ambiguous signs, full of confusion, fear and grief. The believer feels annoyed and irritated. This type of dream has no glad tiding, nor warning, as it is unclear.

A good dream usually comes in the second half of the night, before or after dawn, since it is the time of the angels, and when Allah ﷻ comes nearer to earth. As for a bad dream, it comes in the first part of the night, as it is the time of the devils.

What distinguishes a good dream from other ones are the circumstances and environments in which it came. If the faith of the believer is on the increase; one who makes *Wudu'* before sleeping, recites the *Adhkaar* (remembrance), and sleeps on his right side, then most of the time his dreams would from Allah ﷻ, because he had protected himself from Satan, before sleep.

However, if he is occupied by something and sees it in his dream, then most of the time it would be a *Hadith an-Nafs*. If his faith is on the decrease, and he does not make *Wudu'* before sleeping, nor recite the *Adhkaar*, then he would fall preys to Satan and suffer grief.

In interpreting the verse, **〈they said: "Mixed up dreams; we are not skilled in the interpretation of**

**dreams")** [15], al-Qasimi has said: "Probably they mean false dreams, having no interpretation, because only good dreams carry an interpretation. They also admitted to their lack of knowledge in interpreting dreams. It was as if they had said: 'There is no interpretation for false dreams that we know of.' The king's statement, **(if you can interpret dreams)** [16] is an indication that to his knowledge they were not capable of interpreting dreams, because he used the word '**if**', denoting doubt. Their confirmation that they could not interpret dreams was in agreement with the king's doubt in their level of knowledge about interpreting dreams."[17]

---

[15] Yusuf: Verse 44.
[16] Yusuf: Verse 43.
[17] "*Mahasin at-Ta'weel*", 9/230-231.

# The Benefit of a Good Dream

Aishah, may Allah be pleased with her, said: "The commencement of the Divine Inspiration to Allah's Messenger ﷺ was in the form of good (true) dreams during his sleep. He never had a dream, except that it would come true as the light of day."[18] This Hadith indicates that good dreams are the beginning of the Prophethood.

Al-Hafidh Ibn Hajar, may Allah have Mercy upon him, said: "Ibn Abu Jumrah said: 'A good dream is compared to the brightness of the day because Prophethood was initiated by good dreams, as daylight brightens until the sun rises. Therefore, whoever has a beam of light in his heart, would become truthful and trusting like Abu Bakr, and he whose heart is dark would become blind and a liar like Abu Jahl. The rest of the people fall between these two categories; each according to the light he was given.'"[19]

---

[18] Sahih al-Bukhari: 12/351.
[19] *Fath al-Bari*, 12/355

Anas Ibn Malik reported that the Prophet said: "A good dream (which comes true) of a righteous man is one forty-sixth part of prophethood."[20]

Al-Baghawi has said: "The Prophet's statement '**one forty-sixth part of prophethood**' is confirmation that good dreams are always fulfilled, and that they were a part of the prophethood of the Prophets, but not for anyone else." Ubaid Ibn Umair said: "The dreams of the Prophets were revelations, as he recited Allah's verse, ❨**I have seen in a dream that I was slaughtering you (offered you as a sacrifice to Allah), so what do you think? He said: 'O my father! Do that which you are commanded**❩.

Others, however, have stated that good dreams are one of the signs of prophethood; so the sign of prophethood remains, but Prophethood, itself, does not. The Prophet said: "Good manner of conduct, dignified bearing and moderation are a twenty-fifth part of prophecy."[21]

These noble qualities are a part of the characteristics of the Prophets that righteous people should try to emulate, not because they represent true prophethood, as the prophethood cannot be shared out, nor is there a prophet after Prophet Muhammad.

---

[20] Sahih al-Bukhari: 12/363, Sahih Muslim: 16/23, Imam Malik in his '*Muwatta*': 2/956, al-Baghawi in his '*Sharh as-Sunnah*': 12/203, and Ibn Majah: Hadith No. 3893.
[21] Abu Dawud: 4776 and at-Tirmidhi: 2011, on the authority of Abdullah Ibn Sarjis al-Muzani.

Al-Hafidh Ibn Hajar, may Allah have Mercy upon him, said: "Good dreams (which come true) may also appear to disbelievers, as in the case of the two prisoners with Yusuf ﷺ, and the dream of their king. Al-Qadi, Abu Bakr Ibn al-Arabi has said: 'A dream of a righteous believer is one associated with part of prophethood, one of sincerity and clarity. But, the dream of a sinful disbeliever is not part of prophethood.' Al-Qurtubi said: 'The dream of a righteous sincere Muslim comes true, like one from the Prophets. As for the disbeliever and sinner, their dreams are completely confused, false ones, although their dreams may occasionally come true; this is similar to a liar telling the truth. Not anyone who prophesies is a prophet, such as a diviner or astrologer.'"[22]

## *The Benefit of seeing the Prophet ﷺ in a Dream*

Abu Hurairah ﷺ reported that he heard the Prophet ﷺ say: "Whoever sees me in a dream will see me consciously, as Satan cannot imitate me in appearance."[23]

An-Nawawi, may Allah have Mercy upon him, said: "The above Hadith has three meanings: First, the Prophet ﷺ refers to the people of his era, that whoever sees him in a dream and has not migrated yet, Allah ﷻ would help

---

[22] *Fath al-Bari*: 12/362.
[23] Sahih al-Bukhari: 12/383 and Sahih Muslim: 16/26.

him/her emigrate and therefore see the Prophet ﷺ in person. Second, whoever sees the Prophet ﷺ in a dream in this world, would be able to see him consciously in the Hereafter, because in the Hereafter all of the Ummah of the Prophet ﷺ would see him; those who see him in a dream and even those who do not. Third, whoever sees him ﷺ in a dream, would be able to see him in the Hereafter in person and get his intercession, for Allah knows best."[24]

On the authority of Abu Qatadah ؓ, the Prophet ﷺ said: "Whoever sees me (in a dream), has indeed seen the truth."[25]

Al-Baghawi has said: "It is permissible to see Allah in a dream, because the Prophet ﷺ said, on he authority of Mu'adh ؓ: "I slept and saw my Lord in my dream."[26] Seeing Allah ﷻ in a dream implies that His Justice, Relief, Fertility and Wealth would be in abundance for the people of that area. If one sees Allah ﷻ, promising one Paradise, Forgiveness or Salvation from the Hellfire; then His Words are true and His Promise is always sincere. If one sees Allah ﷻ in a dream looking at one, it implies His Mercy. If one sees Allah, in a dream, ignoring him, it is a warning from sins, as Allah ﷻ has

---

[24] *Sharh an-Nawawi ala Sahih Muslim*: 15/26-27.
[25] Sahih al-Bukhari: 12/383, Sahih Muslim: 10/26 and al-Baghawi: 12/221.
[26] Reported by at-Tirmidhi: 12/115-116 and classified it as Hadith Hassan Sahih, Imam Ahmed: 5/243 and ad-Darami: 2/126 and Albani.

said,

⟨they shall have no portion in the Hereafter (Paradise). Neither will Allah speak to them, nor look at them on the Day of Resurrection⟩ [27]

If one sees Allah, in a dream, giving one wealth from this world and then taking it away from him, it implies that Allah ﷻ has tried one, purified one's soul and showered one with His Mercy.

One would really see the Prophet ﷺ, in a dream, because Satan could not imitate him in appearance. Likewise, one could see other Prophets, Angels, the sun, moon, stars or clouds carrying rain; all of which Satan could not imitate.

If one dreams about angels descending into a place, it could be interpreted as a sign of help and victory for the people of that region, release from suffering, or fertility of the land after a season of drought. Also, if one dreams that an angel is giving one advice, warning or glad tidings, it may be interpreted as receiving honour in this world and is a testimony to one in the Hereafter.

Seeing the Prophet ﷺ in a dream, in a particular place, is interpreted as a sign of relief for the people of that place or region, if they are in a dire situation, a support, if they are oppressed; and it is certainly a relief from suffering. Likewise, seeing the Sahabah, their followers (*Tabi'un*)

---

[27] Al-Imraan: Verse, 77.

or any righteous people in a dream is interpreted as a blessing and good fortune."²⁸

Some scholars have stated that the Hadith, "Whoever sees me in a dream will see me in conscious; for Satan cannot imitate me in appearance," means that a person would see the Prophet ﷺ with the attributes and characteristics with which Allah ﷻ had created him. Al-Bukhari reported that Ibn Sireen had said: "One sees the Prophet ﷺ with his original appearance."

Al-Hafidh, may Allah have Mercy upon him, said: "If someone would tell Muhammad Ibn Sireen that he had seen the Prophet ﷺ in a dream, he would ask him to describe what he had seen in that dream. If the man's description did not fit the Prophet's characteristics, he would tell him, you did not see him." This is confirmed by the Hadith, reported by al-Hakim, on the authority of 'Asem Ibn Kulaib, who quoted his father as saying: "I told Ibn Abbas: 'I saw the Prophet ﷺ in my dream.' Ibn Abbas ؓ replied: 'Describe him to me'. Then, I mentioned al-Hassan Ibn Ali who resembled the Prophet ﷺ. Ibn Abbas ؓ replied: "You have indeed seen him (since al-Hassan Ibn Ali ؓ used to look like the Prophet ﷺ." This Hadith has a good *Isnaad*.

**An Important Lesson**: Al-Hafidh Ibn Hajar said: "One of the benefits of seeing the Prophet ﷺ in a dream is to placate the person who has seen him, as he was certainly

---

²⁸ "*Sharh as-Sunnah*": 12/227-228.

sincere in his love to the Prophet ﷺ." The aforementioned Hadith confirms the statement, "Whoever sees me in a dream will see me in conscious", meaning, whoever has seen him, out of respect, reverence and yearning to see him, has indeed reached his objective and has seen him in wakefulness. The dream might also refer to the Prophet's ﷺ religion and Shari'ah law.

**Another Lesson**: a person must already know the original description of the Prophet ﷺ in order to distinguish which dreams were true and which were imaginations from Satan. From the above authentic Ahadith, the scholars have stated that Satan cannot assume the appearance of the Prophet ﷺ. Not anyone who claims to have seen the Prophet ﷺ has indeed truly seen him; that is why Ibn Sireen used to ask people to describe to him what they had seen.

Therefore, I shall summarize the description of the Prophet ﷺ. He ﷺ was very light skinned, with a broad forehead, large deep black eyes, long eye lashes, long thick beard, broad shoulders, and was neither tall, nor short, curly hair reaching to his shoulders, and if he ﷺ should speak, it would be as if light were coming out from within him.

Ya'qub Ibn Sufyaan quoted Muhammad Ibn Ammar Ibn Yassar as saying: "I asked ar-Rubai', daughter of Mu'wid, 'Describe the Prophet ﷺ to me', she replied: 'O son, if you see him, you would see the sun emerging.' Al-

Bukhari ﷺ reported that Al-Bara' Ibn 'Azib ﷺ was asked: 'Was the Prophet ﷺ like a sword?' He said: 'No, he ﷺ was like the moon.'

# Etiquette of Seeing a Dream

This is the most important part of the book which contains the following three aspects:

A - The Etiquette that a Muslim should adhere to so that his/her dream may come true.

B - The Etiquette that a person should adhere to after having a dream.

C - The Etiquette that interpreters of dreams must adhere to.

## A - The Etiquette that a Muslim should adhere to so that his or her dream may come true

### 1. One must always tell the truth,

The Prophet ﷺ has said: "When the Day of Resurrection approaches, the dreams of a believer would hardly fail to come true; for the most truthful dream would be that of he who was most sincere in his speech."[29]

---

[29] Sahih al-Bukhari: 12/404, Sahih Muslim: 15/20-21, Abu Dawud: 4998, at-Tirmidhi: 9/133, and al-Baghawi: 12/208.

Al-Hafidh Ibn Hajar said: "The Prophet's ﷺ statement, 'When the Day of Resurrection approaches, the dreams of a believer would hardly fail to come true,' indicates three things: First, when most of the religious knowledge would be lost, by the death of scholars, and since further Prophethood is impossible in the Ummah of Islam, after Prophet Muhammad ﷺ, Muslims would therefore be compensated by good dreams, so that some of the religious knowledge, which had been obliterated, would be restored. Second, when the number of believers would decrease, and disbelief, ignorance and moral depravity prevail among people, a believer would then be supported by a good dream as a consolation to him/her. These two statements do not confine to any particular time, but whenever religious knowledge dwindles away, the dreams of sincere believers become true. Third, this could be related to the time of Jesus, son of Mary, ﷺ in particular, and Allah knows best.

As for the Prophet's ﷺ statement: 'for the most truthful dream is that of he who is most sincere in his speech,' Al-Hafidh said: "This happens because a person who is well-known for telling the truth has his heart illuminated, so his power of perception would increase. Therefore, whoever is truthful in wakefulness sees good sincere dreams in his sleep. On the contrary, a liar, whose heart is corrupted and darkened, would only see confused false dreams. Although the opposite may happen, however that is rare, and Allah knows best."[30]

[30] *Fath al-Bari'*, 12/406.

Accordingly, the dreams of the Prophets were always a form of revelation and came true, since they were infallible, being protected from committing wrong actions. Therefore, since the Prophets did not tell lies, unlike most of the Muslims, their dreams always came true.

## 2 - A person should fear Allah ﷻ in all his affairs

Allah ﷻ has promised believers and pious ones glad tidings in this world, saying,
❨ Behold! Verily for the friends of Allah there is no fear, nor shall they grieve; those who believe and keep their duty to Allah. For them are Glad Tidings in the life of the Present, and in the Hereafter ❩ [31]

Glad tidings in the life of this world are that which Allah ﷻ has promised His righteous servants; among these are good dreams, which a believer sees or is shown, as the Prophet ﷺ has said, or the love and praise of people for him/her, as the following Hadith says; on the authority of Abu Darr ؓ, "It was said to Allah's Messenger ﷺ: 'What is your opinion of a person who has done good deeds, whom people admire?' He ﷺ said: 'This is glad tidings

---

[31] Yunus: Verses 62-64.

for a believer (which he/she has received in this world).'"[32]

*Taqwah* (piety) as defined by Imam Ahmad is: "To abandon what you desire for fear of Allah."

## 3 - Muslims should respect the etiquette of sleep

The etiquettes of sleep include:
- One should sleep with good intentions.
- One should sleep in a state of *Taharah* (purity).
- One should repent before one goes to sleep, because one might die during sleep, as Allah ﷻ says,

  ❨**It is Allah that takes the souls (of men) at death: and those that die not (He takes) during their sleep: those on whom He has passed the decree of death He keeps back (from returning to life) but the rest He sends (to their bodies) for an appointed term**❩ [33]

The Prophet ﷺ said: "When anyone of you goes to bed, he should shake out his bed with the inside of his waist sheet, for he does not know what has come on to it after him, and then he should say: '*Bismika Rabbi Wada'tu Janbi wa bika arfa'uhu, In amsakta Nafsi*

[32] Sahih Muslim: 16/189, Imam Ahmad: 5/156-157-168 and Ibn Majah: 4225.
[33] Az-Zumar: Verse 42.

*farhamha wa in arsaltaha fahfazha bima tahfazu bihi ibadakas-salihin.'"* [34] (O my Lord! In your Name I put my side over this bed and with Your Name I will lift it up therefrom. If You take my soul, bestow Mercy on it, and if You release it, protect it as You protect Your Righteous Servants).

If a believer has his soul taken away from him during sleep, he would have died as a repentant servant. Allah ﷻ has said,

⟨**and whoever does not repent, then such are wrong-doers**⟩[35]

Allah ﷻ has divided people into the repentant and the wrongdoers.

A Muslim should not sleep unless his or her will has been written, as reported in a Hadith by Abdullah Ibn Omar ﷺ, in which the Prophet ﷺ said: "It is not permissible for any Muslim, who has something to declare in a will, to stay for more than two nights without having his last will and testament written out and kept ready with him."[36]

A Muslim should sleep on his right side, face the Qiblah and put his hand under his right cheek.

---

[34] Sahih al-Bukhari: 11/126, Sahih Muslim: 17/37, Abu Dawud: 5029 and at-Tirmidhi: 13/78-79.
[35] Al-Hujuraat: Verse 11.
[36] Sahih al-Bukhari: 5/355, Sahih Muslim: 11/74, Imam Malik: 2/761, Abu Dawud: 2845 and an-Nasa'i': 6/238-239.

- One should not make his bed too comfortable and soft, because that would prevent him from waking up to perform night prayers.

- One should protect oneself from Satan and seek Allah's Mercy by reciting the *Adhkaar* for sleeping.

- One should blow on his hands and recite the *Mu'awwidhaat* (Surat al-Falaq and Surat an-Naas) and then pass his hands over his body, as the Prophet ﷺ used to do.

- One should recite Surat *al-Kursi*, as Allah ﷻ would protect him/her from Satan through the night.

- When you go to bed you should say Subhan Allah thirty-three times, Alhamdu lillah thirty-three times and Allahu Akbar thirty-four times. Also one should say: "O my Lord, with Your Name I die and live."

- One should also say, as the Prophet ﷺ did: "O so-and-so, whenever you go to bed say, 'O Allah! I have surrendered myself over to you and have turned my face towards You, and leave all my affairs to You and depend on You and put my trust in You, expecting Your Reward and fearing Your Punishment. There is neither fleeing from You, nor refuge, but with You. I believe in the Book (Qur'an) which You have revealed and in Your Prophet (Muhammad) whom You have sent.'"³⁷

## 4 - One should ask Allah ﷻ to grant him a good dream

Allah has said in the Qur'an,
❮**And your Lord said: "Invoke Me, I will answer your invocation"**❯ ³⁸
and He ﷻ also said,
❮**When my servants ask you concerning Me I am indeed close (to them); I listen to the prayer of every suppliant when he has called on Me**❯³⁹
It is reported that Ai'shah, may Allah be pleased with her, used to say, before going to bed: "O Allah, I ask You to grant me a good dream; a true one, not false; and beneficial, not harmful."

## B - The Etiquette that a person should adhere to after having a dream

**1** - If one sees what one dislikes, such as a dream from Satan, one should spit on one's left side three times, seek refuge with Allah from it and from Satan, and then one should change one's position. If one gets up, its better for

---

³⁷ Sahih al-Bukhari: 11/127, on the authority of Al-Bara' Ibn Azib ؓ

³⁸ Ghafir: Verse 60.
³⁹ Al-Baqarah: Verse 186.

one not to talk about it to anyone, for then it would not harm one, by Allah's Will.

Abu Qatadah ؓ said: I heard Allah's Messenger ﷺ saying, "A good dream is from Allah, and a bad dream is from Satan; so, if anyone of you has had a bad dream which he disliked, then he should spit on his left three times and seek refuge with Allah from it, for then it would not harm him."[40]

An-Nawawi, may Allah have Mercy upon him, said: "The Prophet's statement **'for it would not harm him'**, means that Allah ﷻ has made it (i.e. spitting three times and seeking refuge with Allah) a reason for one's protection and safety, from any harm, if one should have a bad dream, just as He ﷻ has made *Sadaqah* a protection for one's money and a means to ward off affliction. Therefore, if one has a bad dream, one should spit on one's left three times, seek refuge with Allah from Satan, change one's position, and pray two *Rak'at*, if possible."[41]

**2-** If you see a dream that you like, then you should thank Allah ﷻ and narrate it to anyone you like. Abu Sai'd al-Khudri ؓ reported that the Prophet ﷺ said: "If anyone of you sees a dream that he likes, then it is from Allah, and he should thank Allah for it and narrate it to others; but if he sees something else (i.e. a dream that he dislikes), then

---

[40] Sahih al-Bukhari: 12/373, Sahih Muslim: 12/17-18, Ibn Majah: 3909 and Abu Dawud: 5000.
[41] *"Sharh an-Nawawi* on Sahih Muslim", 12/18.

it is from Satan, and he should seek refuge with Allah from its evil, and he should not mention it to anybody, for then it would not harm him."[42]

Abu Razin al-Uqaili ؓ reported that the Prophet ﷺ said: "A believer's dream is a fortieth part of prophecy. It flutters over a man as long as he does not talk about it, but when he talks about it, it settles." And I think he said, "Talk only to a friend or one with sound judgment."[43]

Abu Hurairah ؓ reported that the Prophet ﷺ said: "A dream should not be narrated, except to a scholar or a man with sound judgment."[44]

Al-Hafidh Abu Bakr al-Arabi al-Maliki, may Allah have Mercy upon him, said: "If it is a good dream or you have some doubt about it, do not narrate it except to a scholar or a man with sound judgment."

**3-** You should not narrate your dream to an envier or someone who hates you. Allah ﷻ has said,

❨**Behold Joseph said to his father: "O my father! I did see (in a dream) eleven stars and the sun and the moon: I saw them prostrate themselves to me!" Said (the father): "My (dear) little son! Relate not your vision to your brothers, lest they concoct a plot against you. Verily! Satan is to man an avowed enemy**❩[45]

---

[42] Sahih al-Bukhari: 12/369.
[43] Narrated by at-Tirmidhi: 9/132 and Abu Dawud: 4999.
[44] Narrated by at-Tirmidhi: 9/133.
[45] Yusuf: Verses 4-5.

Al-Qurtubi said: "This is clear proof that a Muslim should warn his fellow Muslim brother of any danger and it is not considered as *Ghaibah* (backbiting), because Jacob ﷺ has warned his son Joseph ﷺ not to narrate his dream to his brothers, lest they devise a plot against him. The Prophet ﷺ said: 'Seek help in secrecy to make your affairs a success, because anyone with good fortune is envied.'[46] In addition, this is clear proof that Jacob ﷺ could interpret dreams, because he knew that his son, Joseph, would be victorious over his brothers, which he did not mind. It shows that a father always wants his son to be better than him, yet someone's own brother would not wish the same for his brother. Jacob ﷺ perceived that his older sons envied Joseph ﷺ, so he ﷺ forbade him to narrate his dream to them, lest they should plan to kill Joseph ﷺ, out of hatred and jealousy."[47]

This is confirmed by the Prophet's Hadith, in which he ﷺ said: "A dream is suspended on a bird's feet unless it is interpreted; as soon as it is interpreted it falls." Shaikh Shams al-Haqq Abadi reported that Al-Khattabi had said: "A dream is undecided until it is interpreted." [48]

---

[46] Narrated by Al-Uqaili in '*adh-Dhoafa*'': 151, at-Tabarani in '*As-Sagheer*', '*Al-Kabeer*' and '*Al-Awsat*' and Abu Nai'm in '*Al-Hilyah*': 5/215, 6/96.
[47] Al-Qurtubi, '*Al-Ja'mi' Li Ahkaam al-Qur'an*': 4/3356.
[48] "*Awn al-Ma'bud Sharh Sunan Abu Dawud*", 13/364.

Moreover, as aforementioned, one has to narrate one's dream to a scholar or a pious person, so that the dream would be interpreted properly.

It is reported in Sahih al-Bukhari, on the authority of Ibn Abbas ﷺ: "A man came to Allah's Messenger and said, 'I saw, in a dream, a cloud giving shade, from which butter and honey were dropping, and I saw people collecting it in their hands; some gathering much and some little. And behold, there was a rope extending from the earth to the sky, and I saw that you (the Prophet) grasped it and ascended, then another man grasped it and ascended, and (after that) another (third) grasped it and ascended, but then when another (fourth) man held it, it broke yet was then re-connected.' Abu Bakr said, 'O Allah's Messenger! Let my father be sacrificed for you! Allow me to interpret this dream.' The Prophet ﷺ said to him, 'Interpret it.' Abu Bakr ﷺ said, 'The cloud with shade symbolizes Islam, and the butter and honey, dropping from it, symbolizes the Qur'an; its sweetness descending; some people will learn much of the Qur'an and others a little. The rope, which is extended from the sky to the earth, is the Truth, which you (the Prophet) are following. You follow it, so Allah will raise you high with it, and then another man would follow it and would rise up with it, and then another person would follow it, and then another man would try to follow it, yet it would break but would then be re-connected for him so that he would also rise up with it. O Allah's Messenger! Let my father be sacrificed for you! Am I right or wrong?' The Prophet ﷺ

replied, 'You are right in part of it, and wrong in another part." Abu Bakr ؓ said, 'O Allah's Prophet! By Allah, you must tell me in what part I was wrong." The Prophet ﷺ said, 'Do not swear.'"

4- You should not claim to have seen a dream which you did not see, because it is considered one of the worst kind of lies. Ibn Abbas ؓ reported that the Prophet ﷺ said, "Whoever claims to have seen a dream which he did not in fact see, would be ordered to make a knot with two barley grains, which he could never do."[49]

Ibn Omar ؓ reported that the Prophet ﷺ said: "The worst lie is that of a person who claims to have seen a dream which he had not seen."[50]

5- One should choose the best time when narrating one's dream to an interpreter. Imam Al-Bukhari had mentioned, in his Sahih, that the best time for the interpretation of dreams is after the *Fajr* prayer. Al-Muhallab has said: "The interpretation of dreams after the *Fajr* prayer is the best and most appropriate time, than any other. This is because a person who had seen a dream could remember it more vividly, with a better presence of mind, before one's daily activities begin to bother one so that the nature of the dream would be apparent. If it was a good one, one could feel glad; but if it was a bad one, one

---

[49] Sahih al-Bukhari: 12/427, Ibn Majah: Hadith No. 3916 and at-Tirmidhi: 9/134-135.
[50] Sahih al-Bukhari: 12/427.

could avoid the negative aspect. Maybe one may dream that one was committing a sin, so one could try to avoid doing it; or it may be a warning against some harm or danger that one could prepare for. These are some of the many advantages of interpreting a dream after the *Fajr* prayer."[51]

## C- The Etiquettes that interpreters of dreams should adhere to

1- The interpreter of dreams must be someone who is righteous and on guard against doing wrong actions at all times, as this kind of knowledge is similar to any other religious knowledge which Allah ﷻ had given to His Prophets and pious ones. Allah ﷻ has said in the Qur'an, with regard to the two prisoners who entered the prison with Yusuf ﷺ,

❨tell us its interpretation; we see that you are of the good-doers❩[52]

They knew that only a good, pious person could interpret dreams correctly, because he would require knowledge and Allah's support. The best interpreters of dreams are Prophets, then their sincere Companions. After Prophet Muhammad ﷺ, the Muslim Ummah has known some famous interpreters of dreams, such as: Abu Bakr as-Siddiq ﷺ, Omar Ibn al-Khattab ﷺ and Ibn Abbas ﷺ. Then, among their followers (the *Ta'bi'un*): Sa'id Ibn al-

---
[51] *"Fath al-Bari"*: 12/440.
[52] Surat Yusuf: Verse 36.

Musayyib and Muhammad Ibn Sireen, who were also scholars as well as having been pious and righteous.

2- The interpreter of dreams must be knowledgeable about the Qur'an, the Sunnah of Prophet Muhammad ﷺ, Arabic language, the culture of a people and their traditions and proverbs. He should also know their social and environmental conditions, characteristics, physical appearance, social attitudes, climate, etc.

3- ʿAbdulghani an-Nabulsi has said: "When told about a dream, the interpreter of dreams should start by saying: 'You have seen a good dream, so we seek Allah's protection from any evil; goodness is for us, and badness is for our enemy; praise be to Allah, the Lord of the worlds. Now you may relate your dream.'"[53] He should also keep things confidential, by not informing anyone, listen carefully with understanding, being aware of the various social groups prevalent in his society, and then take his time when interpreting the dream.[54]

4- The interpreter should not inform anybody about another's dream, unless he was given permission to do so, because of the sense of trust established between him and the dreamer.

---

[53] *"Ta'teer al-Anaam Fi Tafseer al-Ahlaam"*: 1/6.
[54] *"Muntakhab al-Kalaam fi Tafseer al-Ahlaam,"* Muhammad Ibn Sireen, 1/10.

5- Most importantly, he should distinguish between dreams of kings and governors and the common people, because dreams differ according to person's status and position in society; for instance, if a servant dreams about something which he does not deserve, it should be interpreted as belonging to his owner, since he (the servant) owns nothing.[55]

6- An-Nabulsi said: "The interpreter should not rush to interpret dreams until he knows their content, significance and purpose, and asks the person about himself, his people, status, job and livelihood. He should be aware of anything that could possibly help him to interpret the dream more effectively." [56]

7- The interpreter should use the best and most eloquent language possible. It was reported that a Caliph called for an interpreter and asked him: 'I have seen in a dream that all my teeth fell out.' The interpreter said: 'All your relatives will die.' The Caliph's face changed and was furious; so he called for another interpreter and related his dream to him, the second interpreter said: 'If the dream of my Caliph comes true, he will live longer than his relatives.' The caliph was happy and so rewarded him. Both interpretations were correct however, yet the approach was different.

---

[55] *"Muntakhab al-Kalaam fi Tafseer al-Ahlaam,"* Muhammad Ibn Sireen.
[56] *"Ta'teer al-Anaam"*: 2/353.

8- The interpreter should thank Allah ﷻ if he succeeds in interpreting a dream, rather than displaying conceit or arrogance; for Yusuf ﷺ said:

❮ O my Lord! You have indeed bestowed on me some power and taught me something of the interpretation of dreams and events❯(12: 101).

# Categories of Interpreting Dreams

## A- Interpreting Dreams from a Qur'anic Perspective

Al-Baghawi, may Allah ﷻ have Mercy upon him, said: "Dreams may be interpreted by the Qur'an, as in the case of someone who dreams of a rope, which may be interpreted as a **Covenant**, as Allah ﷻ has said,
⟨**and hold fast, all of you together, to the Rope of Allah**⟩ (3: 103),
that is the Covenant of Allah ﷻ.

## A Ship

A Ship may be interpreted as a rescue, as Allah ﷻ has said,
⟨**then We saved him and those with him in the ship**⟩ (29: 15).

## Wood

Wood may be interpreted as hypocrisy, because Allah ﷻ has said in *Surat Al-Munafiqun*, with regard to the hypocrites,
❴and when you look at them, their bodies please you; and when they speak, you listen to their words. They are as blocks of wood, propped up❵ (63: 4).

## Stones

Stones may be interpreted as hardness, as Allah ﷻ has said,
❴then, after that, your hearts were hardened and became as stones or even harder❵ (2: 74).

## Disease

A disease or a sick person may be interpreted as hypocrisy. Allah ﷻ has said,
❴in their hearts is a disease (of doubt and hypocrisy)❵ (2: 10).

## Eggs

Eggs may be interpreted as women, as in Allah's Verse,
❴as if they were eggs well preserved❵ (37: 49),
and also garments or body covers are interpreted as women, as Allah has said in *Surat al-Baqarah*,
❴They (women) are your garments❵ (2: 187).

## Water

**Water** or rain is interpreted as *Fitnah* (trial and a test) in some cases, as Allah ﷻ has said,
❴**We should surely have bestowed on them rain in abundance that We might try them thereby**❵ (72: 16-17).

## Meat

The eating of meat may be interpreted as *Ghaibah* (backbiting); as Allah ﷻ has said,
❴**Would one of you like to eat the flesh of his dead brother?**❵ (49: 12).

## The Entry of a King

The entry of a king into a house, city or a country, which is of less importance to him, may be interpreted as a disaster or humiliation that may befall its people, as Allah has said,
❴**Kings when they enter a town despoil it and make the noblest of its people its lowest**❵ (27: 34).

## Ascension to the Sky

Ascension to the sky may be interpreted as acquiring high rank, as Allah ﷻ has said,
❴**and We raised him to a high station**❵ (19: 57)

Al-Baghawi has said: "Whoever dreams of rising to the sky and entering it, would be honoured and achieve martyrdom".[57] He also said: "Dreaming of washing one's body and making ablution with cold water may be interpreted as making repentance, being cured from a disease, released from prison, discharged of having to pay a debt, and being safeguarded from fear. However, washing one's body fully is an even stronger sign than ablution; Allah ﷻ had said to Ayyub ﷺ (Job),

❨This is a spring of water to wash in; a cool and (refreshing) water❩ (38: 42).

So, when Ayyub ﷺ washed himself, all his loathsome sores were removed from him. Dreaming of washing oneself and making ablution with hot water may be interpreted as a sign of distress or disease.

## Adhan

Dreaming of making *Adhan* may be interpreted as performing *Hajj*, as Allah ﷻ has said,

❨and proclaim to mankind the *Hajj*❩ (22: 27).

## Ruku

Dreaming of making *Ruku'* (bowing) may be interpreted as a sign of one's repentance; Allah ﷻ has said,

❨and he fell down prostrate and turned to Allah in repentance❩ (37: 24).

---

[57] *"Sharh as-Sunnah"*, 12/220-221.

## Sujud

Dreaming of making *Sujud* (prostration) may be interpreted as one's drawing near to Allah, as He ﷻ has said,

❲**make *Sujud* and draw near to Allah**❳ (96: 19).

## Praying with the wrong Qiblah

Dreaming of offering prayers in the wrong direction of the *Qiblah*, East or West, may be interpreted as a sign of one's deviation from the Sunnah of Prophet Muhammad ﷺ. If one prays with his back facing the *Qiblah*, it may be interpreted as a rejection of Islam, as Allah ﷻ has said,
❲**but they threw it away behind their backs**❳ (2: 187).
If one dreams that one did not know the direction of the *Qiblah*, it may be interpreted that one is confused with regard to one's religion (Islam). If one dreams that one is praying on top of the *Ka'bah*, it may be interpreted as a sign that one may abandon one's religion. We seek refuge with Allah ﷻ from that.

## The Ka'bah

Dreaming of the *Ka'bah* may be interpreted as a sign of a just ruler and whoever dreams of making *Tawaf* (circumambulation) around the *Ka'bah* or performing some rites of the pilgrimage, may be interpreted as a sign of one's righteousness in one's religion, according to one's deeds. Dreaming of a mosque may be interpreted as a sign of becoming a ruler.

## Entering Makkah

Dreaming of entering *Makkah* may be interpreted as a sign of security, because Allah ﷻ has said,
❨**whosoever enters it attains security**❩ (3: 97).

## Offering a Sacrifice

If a servant dreamed of offering to slaughter an animal as a sacrifice, it may be interpreted as a sign of his emancipation. Likewise if he were a prisoner, it may be interpreted as a sign of his rescue; but as a sign of security if he were afraid, discharge of his debt if he were indebted, cure if he were sick, and going on pilgrimage if he had not yet performed *Hajj*.[58]

## The Day of Judgement

Al-Baghawi also said: "Whoever dreams that the Day of Judgement is established at a certain place, may have his dream interpreted as a sign that justice would be extended to that place. If they have been mistreated and oppressed, they would be made victorious, but if they had been unjust oppressors, Allah would take revenge against

---

[58] "*Sharh as-Sunnah*", 12/235-236.

them, because the Day of Judgement is considered as the Day of Justice and the Final Decision. Allah ﷻ has said, ❨and We shall set up balances of justice on the Day of Resurrection, then none would be dealt with unjustly, in anything❩ (21: 47).

## Entering the Paradise

Whoever dreams of entering Paradise, may take this as the glad tidings from Allah ﷻ that one will enter Paradise. If one should dream of eating some of its food, it may be interpreted as a beneficial thing; that one will attain much in one's religion and in the world, and gain knowledge which would avail one. However, if one dreams of giving it to someone else, it may be interpreted as a sign that someone else would benefit from his knowledge.

## Entering the Hellfire

Dreaming of entering the Hellfire may be interpreted as a warning to a sinner, from one's sins and wrong deeds, in order that one should repent. If one dreams that one is eating some of Hellfire's food or drink, it may be interpreted as contrary to one's good deeds or knowledge, which would produce evil consequences for one.

## Cows

Dreaming of healthy fat cows may be interpreted as fertile years; if they are lean, it may be interpreted as s sign of barren years of harvest. Allah ﷻ has said, with regard to the story of Yusuf ﷺ,

**❨then will come after that seven severe years, which would devour what you have laid by, in advance for them❩** (12: 48)

Yusuf ﷺ interpreted the devouring of the fat cows by the lean ones as difficult infertile years, which would devour what would have been put aside, in advance of them, during the fertile years.

## Parents

It is stated that if a person dreams that one's parents are displeased with one, it indicates that Allah ﷻ is displeased with one, because Allah has said,

**❨give thanks to Me and to your parents❩** (31: 14)

In some narration, it is said: "If Allah is pleased with someone, it means that his parents are pleased with him, and if Allah is displeased with someone, it means that his parents are displeased with him."

## Allah's Anger

Also if someone dreams that Allah ﷻ is angry with him, it may be interpreted that he would fall from a high place. Allah ﷻ has said,

❨he on whom My Anger descends, he is indeed perished❩ (20: 81).

## Salaah

Whoever dreams of performing obligatory *Salaah*, may have the dream interpreted as a sign that one would perform the *Hajj* and avoid evil deeds, because Allah has said,

❨Verily, Salah prevents one from doing evil deeds and iniquity❩ (29: 45).

## A Dead Person

Dreaming of seeing a dead person that one knows and informs him that he has not died, may be interpreted as a sign that the dead person is in a good situation in the Hereafter, as Allah ﷻ has said,

❨Nay, they are alive, with their Lord, and they have provision❩ (3: 169).

Likewise, if one dreams of a dead person laughing, it is interpreted that one would be forgiven, as Allah has said,

❨Some faces that Day will be bright laughing, rejoicing at good news (of Paradise)❩ (80: 38-39).

## Hellfire

Scholars have said: "Any dream of Hellfire is an indication of an immediate *Fitnah*, as Allah ﷻ has said, ❨

Taste you your trial! This is what you used to ask to be hastened⟫ (51: 14)."

## Old Age

Dreaming of having reached old age, bowing one's head, may be interpreted as having a long life, as Allah has said, ⟪and he whom We granted long life, We reverse him in creation (weakness after strength). Will they not then understand?⟫ (36: 68).

## Perfume

Dreaming of taking a bottle of perfume and putting it on someone, may be interpreted as a sign that one is pliant, as Allah ﷻ has said,
⟪their desire is that you should be pliant; so would they be pliant⟫ (68: 9).

## Play

Dreaming of playing with anything may be interpreted as something abominable, because Allah ﷻ has said,
⟪did the people of the towns then feel secure against the coming of Our Punishment, in the forenoon while they play?⟫ (7: 98).

## A Shirt

Dreaming of a shirt may be interpreted as glad tidings, as Allah ﷻ has said
❨Go with this shirt of mine❩ (12: 93)
It may also be interpreted as a man for a woman, and a woman for a man, as Allah has said,
❨They are your garments and you are the same for them❩ (2: 187)
However, if he dreams that his shirt or garment is torn, it may be interpreted as a sign of someone divorcing his wife. A white shirt may be interpreted as a man's honour, pride and religion.

## Death

Dreaming that one dies and is placed in a grave, may be interpreted that he would go on a long journey, as Allah ﷻ has said,
❨then He causes him to die, and puts him in his grave. Then, when it is His Will, He will resurrect him again❩ (80: 21-22).

## Entering a Door

Dreaming that one is entering by a door may be interpreted that one would be triumphant if one were in a dispute with someone, as Allah has said,
❨Enter in upon them by the gate, for if you enter by it, you would be victorious❩ (5: 23).

## A Bird Flying Overhead

If one dreams that a bird is flying over one's head, it may indicate that one would acquire leadership, as Allah has said,
⟨**and the birds gathered: all were obedient to him (turning to Allah**⟩ (38: 19).

## Speaking to a Leader

If one dreams that a governor or leader is speaking to one, it may be interpreted as a sign that one would reach a high rank or status, as Allah ﷻ has said,
⟨**when he spoke to him, he said: "Verily, this day, you are with us, high in rank and fully trusted."**⟩ (12: 54).

## An Army

If one dreams that an army of soldiers is gathering, it may indicate that the followers of falsehood will be destroyed but the followers of truth will be victorious, as Allah ﷻ has said,
⟨**We verily shall come unto them with hosts that they cannot resist**⟩ (27: 37).

## Peace

Dreaming of making peace indicates that goodness is established, as Allah has said,

❰and making peace is better❱ (4: 128).

## Being Bound

Dreaming that one is bound together, by someone, with fetters, may indicate that one has done some major sins that would result in one's punishment by the ruler, as Allah has said,
❰and you will see the sinners that day bound together in fetters❱ (14: 49).

## Headache

Dreaming of having a headache may be interpreted as a sign that one should repent, give charity, do righteous deeds or stop committing sinful deeds, because Allah ﷻ has said,
❰whoever among you is sick or has an ailment of the head must compensate by fasting, almsgiving or making a (sacrificial) offering❱ (2: 196).

## A Bed

If one dreams that one is buying a bed or sleeping in a bed, it may indicate that an enormous benefit and blessing would be bestowed upon one, as Allah has said,
❰whosoever does righteous deeds, then for such will He prepare a good place (in Paradise)❱ (30: 44).

## Being in a Room

Dreaming of being in a room or rooms may be interpreted as a sign that one would be safe from what one fears, because Allah ﷻ has said,
❨and they will reside in high dwellings (Paradise), in peace and security❩ (34: 37).

## Al-Qisas (Law of Equality)

Dreaming of *al-Qisas* (law of equality) indicates a long life, as Allah has said,
❨In the law of equality there is (a saving of) life for you, O you men of understanding❩ (2: 179).

## Drinking Alcohol

Whoever dreams that he is drinking alcohol and no one is fighting with him over it, it may be interpreted as a sign that he would gain an illegal fortune, according to the amount of alcohol that he had drunk; it may also be interpreted as great sin, as Allah ﷻ has said,
❨They ask you concerning alcoholic drink and gambling. Say: "In them there is great sin."❩ (2: 219).

## The Waves of the Sea

Dreaming of sea waves may be interpreted as a punishment or hardship, as Allah has said,

⟨and when a wave covers them like shades, they invoke Allah, making their invocations for Him only⟩ (31: 32) and He ﷻ has said,
⟨and a wave came between them, so he was among those who drowned⟩ (11: 43).

## Couches

Dreaming of couches may be interpreted as rest or leadership, as Allah has said,
⟨reclining upon the couches lined with silk brocade⟩ (55: 54).
This may also be interpreted as a sign of women and children, as Allah ﷻ has said in *Surat al-Wa'qi'ah*,
⟨and on couches, raised high. Verily, We have created them (maidens) of special creation. And made them virgins, beloved, equal in age⟩ (56: 34-37).

## Divorce

Dreaming of divorcing one's wife may be interpreted as a sign that one would receive provision in abundance, as Allah ﷻ has said,
⟨but if they separate (by divorce), Allah will provide, in abundance, for everyone of them, from His Bounty⟩ (4: 130).

## Treating a Person Unjustly

Dreaming that one is treating someone unjustly, may be interpreted that that person would be triumphant; similarly, if one dreams that someone is treating one unjustly, because Allah has said,
❴To those against whom war is made, permission is given (to fight), because they are wronged, and verily Allah is Most powerful in their aid❵ (22: 39).

## White Eyes

Dreaming that one's eyes have become white indicates long suffering in sorrow, as Allah ﷻ has said, with regard to Yaqub ؑ,
❴And his eyes became white with sorrow, and he fell into silent melancholy❵ (12: 84).

## Blindness

Dreaming that one's eyes have gone blind may be interpreted as a sign that one would abandon Islam, as Allah has said,
❴and whoever is blind in this world will be blind in the Hereafter, and more astray from the Path❵ (17: 72).
Some scholars have also interpreted this as referring to someone who memorises the Qur'an, but then forgets it.

## Biting the Fingers

Dreaming of someone biting the tips of one's fingers may be interpreted as a sign that one is full of hatred, because Allah ﷻ has said
⟨they bite the tips of their fingers at you in rage⟩ (3: 119).
Other scholars have interpreted this as being a wrongdoer, as Allah has said,
⟨the Day when the wrongdoer will bite at his hands⟩ (25: 27).

## Sleep

Dreaming of slumber may be interpreted as a sign of security, as Allah ﷻ has said,
⟨when He covered you with slumber, as a security from Him⟩ (8: 11).

## A Pledge

Dreaming of being a pledge is interpreted that one has committed many evil deeds, as Allah has said,
⟨every soul is a pledge for its own deeds⟩ (74: 38)

## The Sky

Dreaming that the sky is being built in his presence indicates that one gives false testimony, as Allah ﷻ has said,

❨I made them not to witness the creation of the heavens and the earth❩ (18: 51).

## A Camel Entering

Dreaming that a camel is entering a place may be interpreted as a sign that a *Fitnah* would befall that place, because Allah ﷻ has said,
❨verily, We are sending the she-camel as a test for them❩ (54: 27).

## A Gift

Dreaming of a gift indicates happiness, because Allah has said in the Qur'an
❨you rejoice in your gift❩ (27: 36).

## Booty of War

Dreaming of taking war booty is interpreted that one's earning is illegal, as Allah has said,
❨It is not for any Prophet to take illegally any part of booty, so whoever deceives his companions as regards the booty, he shall bring forth on the Day of Resurrection that which he took illegally❩ (3: 161).

# B- Interpreting Dreams from the Perspective of the Hadith of Prophet Muhammad ﷺ

## A Crow or a Mouse

Al-Baghawi, may Allah have Mercy upon him: "Dreams may also be interpreted from a Hadith perspective, such as: dreaming of a crow is interpreted as a sign of sinful person, because the Prophet ﷺ said so, and dreaming of a mouse is interpreted as a sign of a sinful woman because the Prophet ﷺ said so.

## Ribs

Dreaming of ribs may be interpreted as a sign of women, because the Prophet ﷺ has said: "Treat women nicely, for a women is created from a rib, and the most curved portion of the rib is its upper portion; if you should try to straighten it, it will break, but if you leave it as it is, it will remain crooked. So treat women nicely." [59]

## Glass Vessels

Dreaming of glass vessels may also be interpreted as a sign of women because once, when the Prophet ﷺ was on a journey, his servant, called Anjasha, was driving the camels (too fast, while there were women riding on

---

[59] Sahih al-Bukhari: 6/363, Ibn Majah: 525, Imam Ahmad: 5/8 and ad-Darami: 2/148.

them). So, Allah's Messenger ﷺ said, "*Waihaka* (May Allah be merciful to you), O Anjasha! Drive the camels slowly with those glass vessels (women)!"⁶⁰

# Milk

Dreaming of milk may be interpreted as a sign of having knowledge or a good natural disposition. Ibn Omar ؓ said: "I heard the Prophet ﷺ saying: 'While I was sleeping, I saw that a cupfull of milk being brought to me, so I drank my fill till I noticed its (i.e. the milk's) wetness coming out of my nails. Then, I gave the remaining milk to Omar Ibn Al-Khattab.' The Companions of the Prophet ﷺ asked, 'What have you interpreted (from this dream), O Allah's Messenger?' He ﷺ replied, '(It is religious) knowledge.'"⁶¹

Al-Hafidh Ibn Hajar, may Allah have Mercy upon him, said: "In some narrations milk is interpreted as *Fitrah* (one's natural disposition). Al-Bazzar has reported: "Dreaming of milk may be interpreted as one's natural disposition." At-Tabarani narrated: "Whoever dreams of drinking milk, it may be interpreted as *Fitrah*." In Sahih al-Bukhari, Abu Hurairah ؓ reported: "When the Prophet ﷺ took the cup of milk, Jibreel ؑ said: 'Praise be to Allah Who guides you to the *Fitrah*.'"⁶²

---

⁶⁰ Sahih al-Bukhari: 10/538 and Imam Ahmad: 3/107-117.
⁶¹ Sahih al-Bukhari: 12/393, at-Tirmidhi: 9/135-136 and ad-Darami: 2/128.
⁶² "*Fat'h al-Bari*": 12/393 and the last Hadith is in Sahih al-Bukhari: 10/70.

## Shirts

Dreaming of shirts indicates religion; Abu Sai'd al-Khudri ❖ reported that the Prophet ﷺ said: "While I was sleeping I saw (in a dream) some people wearing shirts, of which some were reaching up to the breasts only while others were even shorter than that. Omar Ibn Al-Khattab was shown wearing a shirt which was dragging." The people asked, "How did you interpret it O Allah's Messenger?" He (the Prophet ﷺ) replied, "It is the *Deen* (Religion)."[63]

Al-Hafidh Ibn Hajar said: "Shirts are interpreted as one's religion because normally shirts cover one's body in this world, and religion protects it in the Hereafter, from any harm. This is confirmed by Allah's Verse,

**⟨O you children of Adam! We have bestowed raiment upon you to cover your shame, as well as to be an adornment for you, but the raiment of righteousness is the best⟩** (7: 26).

Arabs also use the word 'raiment or clothing' to refer to piety and kindness. The Prophet ﷺ said to Uthman Ibn Affan ❖: "Perhaps Allah will clothe you with a shirt, Uthman, but if the people want you to take it off, do not take it off for them."[64]

---

[63] Sahih al-Bukhari: 12/395, at-Tirmidhi: 9/137 al-Baghawi in his book '*Sharh as-Sunnah*': 12/241 and ad-Darami: 2/127.
[64] Narrated by Imam Ahmad, at-Tirmidhi, Ibn Majah and Ibn Hibban.

Scholars have agreed that dreaming of a shirt is interpreted as the *Deen* (religion); the length of the shirt indicates the effect of the religion after the person's death. However, this is only as far as dreaming of shirts is concerned, since dragging one's long shirt in wakefulness is prohibited."[65]

## Fettered Feet

Dreaming of fetters on one's feet may be interpreted as a sign of one's firm adherence to religion. The Prophet ﷺ has said: "I love fetters but hate iron collars, as fetters are firm adherence to religion."[66]

An-Nawawi, may Allah have Mercy upon him, said: "Scholars have said: 'The Prophet ﷺ likes fetters on the feet because they symbolize one's abstention from sins and evil acts; as for an iron collar, it is normally placed around one's neck and is a characteristic of the People of the Hellfire. Allah ﷻ has said,
⟨verily! We have put iron collars around their necks⟩ (36: 8)
and
⟨when iron collars will be fixed around their necks⟩ (40: 71)."[67]

---

[65] "*Fat'h al-Bari*": 12/396.
[66] Sahih al-Bukhari.
[67] "*Sharh an-Nawawi ala' Sahih Muslim*": 12/22-23.

## Water

Kharijah Ibn Zaid has said: Umm Al-'Ala, an *Ansari* woman, who had given a pledge of allegiance to Allah's Messenger told me, "The *Muhajirun* (emigrants) were divided amongst us by drawing lots, and we got 'Uthman Ibn Madhrun as our share. We made him stay with us in our house. But then he suffered from a disease which proved fatal. When he died and was given a bath and was shrouded in his clothes. Allah's Messenger came, and I said, (addressing the dead body), 'O Abu As-Sa'ib! May Allah be Merciful to you! I testify that Allah has honoured you.' Allah's Messenger remarked, 'How do you know that Allah has honoured him?' I replied, 'Let my father be sacrificed for you, O Allah's Messenger! On whom else shall Allah bestow His honour?' Allah's Messenger said, 'As for him, by Allah, death has come to him. By Allah, I wish him nothing but good (from Allah). By Allah, in spite of the fact that I am Allah's Messenger, I do not even know what Allah will do to him, nor to me.' "Umm Al-'Ala added, 'By Allah, I will never attest the righteousness of anybody after that.' She added, 'Later I saw in a dream, a flowing spring for 'Uthman. So I went to Allah's Messenger and mentioned that to him. He ﷺ replied, 'That is (the symbol of) his good deeds.'"[68]

Al-Baghawi, may Allah have Mercy upon him, said: "The Prophet ﷺ has interpreted a flowing spring as an ongoing, good deed. On the other hand, dreaming of a

---
[68] Sahih al-Bukhari: 12/410 and al-Baghawi: *'Sharh as-Sunnah'*: 12/242-243.

small stream may be interpreted as a good life; sea may be interpreted as a powerful king, if one dreams that one is drinking from it, it may be interpreted that one will get wealth from the king; dreaming of drinking from clear water may be interpreted as a sign of receiving a blessing and a good life. If it is turbid water, it may be interpreted as a disease inflicted upon someone. Dreaming of drinking hot water and entering the bathroom may be interpreted as a sign of sickness and distress."[69]

Dreaming of a falling rain may be interpreted as Mercy from Allah ﷻ. However, if it falls in a particular place, it may be interpreted as s sign of diseases that would strike that place.

Dreaming of mud and dirty water may be interpreted as a sign of distress and grief; flood and torrential stream may be interpreted as a dominating enemy; snow, coldness and ice as punishment and grief; swimming in a pool is interpreted as one's impediment in something; walking on water may be interpreted as strength and certainty; dreaming of a water covering may be interpreted as severe grief; dreaming of drowning in water and staying alive may be interpreted as being immersed in worldly affairs; dreaming of water leaking from the house walls may be interpreted as sorrow, infliction and crying.

In general dreaming of water is good and a bucket is an indication of one's luck. Ibn Omar ﷺ reported that the

---

[69] Al-Baghawi's '*Sharh as-Sunnah*': 12/244-245.

Prophet ﷺ said: "While (in a dream), I was standing by a well, drawing water from it, Abu Bakr and Omar came to me. Abu Bakr took the bucket (from me) and drew one or two buckets of water, and then he showed some weakness in his pulling; May Allah forgive him. Then Ibn Al-Khattab took the bucket from Abu Bakr, and the bucket turned into a very large one in his hands. I had never seen such a mighty person amongst the people as him, in performing such hard work. He drew so much water that the people drank to their satisfaction and watered their camels."[70]

The Prophet's statement 'Abu Bakr took the bucket (from me) and drew one or two buckets of water' is an indication of his short period as Caliph (only two years). His statement with regard to Omar Ibn al-Khattab ؓ, 'and the bucket turned into a very large one in his hands', is an indication of his long period as Caliph, and the security and conquest of many countries during his reign. The Prophet's saying, 'He drew so much water that the people drank to their satisfaction and watered their camels', is an indication that the Muslim lands expanded, disputes ceased, wealth was in abundance and people lived peacefully, leading lives of plenty and opulence, during his reign."[71]

Al-Hafidh Ibn Hajar said: "Dreaming of drawing water from a well indicates that one will be appointed as a

---

[70] Sahih al-Bukhari: 12/412 ands at-Tirmidhi: 9/144-145.
[71] "*A'rida al-Ahudit*": 9/155-157.

governor of a district or province. His period in office will be according to the amount of water he has drawn. Dreaming of a well may also be interpreted as a woman, and the number of children she will give birth to."[72]

## Keys

Dreaming of holding keys in one's hand may be interpreted as wealth, power and authority. Abu Hurairah ؓ narrated that the Prophet ﷺ said: "I have been given the keys of eloquent speech and given victory with awe (cast into the hearts of the enemy), and while I was sleeping last night, the keys of the treasures of the earth were brought to me, till they were placed in my hand."[73]

Al-Hafidh Ibn Hajar said: "Keys are interpreted as wealth, authority and power. Whoever dreams of opening a door with a key, he will attain his goal with the help of someone powerful, and if he dreams that he is holding keys in his hand, he will achieve authority and power."[74]

## A Palace

Dreaming of a palace indicates one's good deeds for religious people, but a prison for others. Abu Hurairah ؓ reported that the Prophet ﷺ said: "While we were in the

---

[72] "*Fat'h al-Bari*": 12/415.
[73] Sahih al-Bukhari: 12/401 and Sahih Muslim: 4/5.
[74] "*Fat'h al-Bari*": 12/401 and an-Nasa'i': 6/3-4.

company of the Prophet ﷺ, he said, 'While I was asleep, I saw myself in Paradise and there I beheld a woman making ablution beside a palace. I asked, 'To whom does this palace belong?' They said, 'To Omar Ibn Al-Khattab.' Then I remembered Omar's *Ghairah* (concerning women), and so I quickly went away from that palace.' (When Omar heard this from the Prophet ﷺ), he wept and said, 'Do you think it is likely that I feel *Ghairah* because of you, O Allah's Messenger?'"[75]

Al-Hafidh Ibn Hajar said: "Interpreters of dreams have said that dreaming of a palace is interpreted as one's good deeds for religious people, but a prison or depression for others. Dreaming of entering a palace may also be interpreted as one's getting married."[76]

## Wudu (Ablution)

Al-Hafidh also said: "Interpreters of dreams have also stated that dreaming of making Ablution (*Wudu'*) is interpreted as a means to achieve authority or a goal. If one finishes it in his dream, one would attain his objective in waking; however, if one could not finish his ablution in one's dream, because of the shortage of water or because one had used impure water, one's goals would not be achieved. Dreaming of making ablution is a sign of security for a fearful person, and it also indicates a reward and an expiation of sins."[77]

---

[75] Sahih al-Bukhari: 12/415.
[76] "*Fat'h al-Bari*": 12/416.
[77] "*Fat'h al-Bari*": 12/417.

## Tawaf around the Ka'bah

Dreaming of performing *Tawaf* around the *Ka'bah* indicates that one will go on *Hajj*. Ibn Omar ؓ reported that Allah's Messenger ﷺ said, "While I was sleeping, I saw myself performing the *Tawaf* of the *Ka'bah*. Behold, there I saw a pale red long-haired man (supporting himself) between two men, with water dripping from his hair. I asked, 'Who is this?' The people replied, 'He is the son of Mary.' Then I turned my face to see another man with a red complexion, big body, curly hair, and was blind in the right eye, which looked like a protruding out grape. I asked, 'Who is he?' They replied, 'He is Ad-Dajjal.' Ibn Qatatan resembles him more than anybody else among the people; Ibn Qattaan was a man from Bani Al-Mustaliq from Khuza'ah."[78]

Al-Hafidh Ibn Hajar said: "Interpreters of dreams have stated that dreaming of performing *Tawaf* around the *Ka'bah* indicates that one could go on *Hajj*, get married, achieve something from a ruler, show kindness to one's parents, be at the service of a scholar or undertake a task."

---

[78] Sahih al-Bukhari: 12/147.

## A Sword

Dreaming of a sword may be interpreted as the help and support which one requires for a battle. Abu Musa' ؓ reported that the Prophet ﷺ said, "In a dream I saw myself emigrating from Makkah to a place with plenty of date trees. I thought that it was Al-Yamamah or Hajar, but it turned out to be Madinah, (Yathrib). In the same dream I saw myself moving a sword but its blade broke. It came to symbolize the defeat, which the Muslims suffered, on the Day of Uhud. I moved the sword again, and it became whole as before, and that was the symbol of the victory Allah bestowed upon Muslims and their uniting together. I saw cows in my dream, and by Allah, that was a blessing, as they symbolized the believers on the Day of Uhud. That blessing was the good Allah bestowed upon us, and the reward of true belief which Allah gave us after the day of Badr."[79]

An-Nawawi said: "Interpreters of dreams have stated that the Prophet ﷺ interpreted his dream as such, because the sword of a man is normally interpreted as his supporters who back him. In another occasion, a sword can also be interpreted as one's children, father, wife, uncle or brother. It also refers to authority, trust, a man's eloquence, or an unjust ruler. It all depends on the circumstances and combined factual evidence of the person who had the dream, or of the nature of dream itself.

---

[79] Sahih al-Bukhari: 12/421, Sahih Muslim: 15/31-32 and Ibn Majah: Hadith No. 3921.

## Cows

The Prophet's 🕊 statement: "I saw cows in my dream, and by Allah, that was a blessing, and they symbolized the believers on the Day of Uhud. That blessing was the good Allah bestowed upon us and the reward of true belief which Allah gave us after the day of Badr", can be interpreted by adding Imam Muslim's part of a similar Hadith, that is missing in Imam al-Bukahri's Hadith, that is, '**I saw cows being slaughtered there**'; therefore, those cows slaughtered proved to symbolize the Followers 🕊 who were killed on the Day of the battle of Uhud."[80]

## Blowing

Dreaming of blowing indicates that the things blown at will vanish, without much effort. Abu Hurairah 🕊 narrated that the Prophet 🕊 said: "While I was sleeping, I was given the treasures of the earth and two gold bracelets were placed in my hands, and I did not like that, but I received the inspiration that I should blow on them, and I did so, and both of them vanished. I interpreted it as referring to the two liars between whom I am present; the ruler of San'a and the ruler of Yamamah."[81]

---

[80] "*Sharh an-Nawawi ala' Sahih Muslim*": 15/32.
[81] Sahih al-Bukhari: 12/423, Sahih Muslim: 15/34, at-Tirmidhi: 9/154-155 and Ibn Majah: Hadith No. 3922.

Ibn Battal said: "Interpreters of dreams stated that dreaming of blowing indicates that the things blown at vanish without much effort and refers to speech. Allah ﷻ destroyed the two mentioned liars, by the Prophet's words, and then ordered him to kill them."[82]

## Gold

Al-Hafidh reported that al-Qadi Iyyad, may Allah have Mercy upon him, said: "Since the Prophet ﷺ dreamt that the two bracelets were placed on his hands and he ﷺ was in the middle, he ﷺ interpreted them as not being in their proper place because gold is not an ornament for men; likewise, a liar tells fabrications and falsehood. Therefore, since the two bracelets were made of gold, it indicates that the rulers of San'a and Yamamah would be destroyed."

Al-Qurtubi said: "As for the Prophet's dream concerning the two bracelets, it means that the people of San'a and Yamamah embraced Islam and were a great support for Islam. However, when the two liars came to power and became rulers of the two tribes, they eloquently lied to people and managed to convince them with their falsehood and deceit, so the people believed them. The two hands mentioned in the Prophet's dream symbolizes the two tribes, the two bracelets symbolize the two liars,

---

[82] "*Fat'h al-Bari*": 12/423.

and being of gold is an indication of their flowery speech."[83]

## Marriage

Dreaming of marrying a particular woman may be interpreted as attaining a position of power, according to the woman's beauty. Others have stated that would marry her in real life, or someone who looks like her. Ai'shah, may Allah be pleased with her, reported that the Prophet ﷺ told her, "You have been shown to me twice in my dreams. I saw you pictured on a piece of silk and someone said (to me). 'This is your wife.' When I uncovered the picture, I saw that it was yours. I said, 'If this is from Allah, it will be done.'"[84]

Al-Baghawi said: "Dreaming of marrying a woman whom one knows, or is acquainted with or related to may be interpreted as attaining a position of power, according to her beauty. If he does not know her, nor is he related to her, but he named her as his bride in his dream, it may be interpreted as his death or that he will kill someone. Dreaming of committing illegal intercourse with a whore may be interpreted as gaining illegal wealth. If a woman dreams of getting married, it may be interpreted as having

---

[83] "*Fat'h al-Bari*": 12/424.
[84] Sahih al-Bukhari: 12/400, Sahih Muslim: 15/202 and al-Baghawi's '*Sharh as-Sunnah*': 12/236.

a good life, and if she dreams of marrying a dead man, her wealth will decrease and her life will be ruined."[85]

## Silky Clothes

Women's dreaming of silky clothes may be interpreted as their getting married, acquiring wealth, experiencing a ceremony of mourning, or getting fat. It has been stated that clothes are the mirror of a person, because they epitomise their status.[86]

## Clouds

Dreaming of clouds is interpreted as wisdom, and honey and butter as the Qur'an and Sunnah of Prophet Muhammad ﷺ. It is reported in Sahih al-Bukhari, on the authority of Ibn Abbas ؓ: "A man came to Allah's Messenger and said, 'I saw, in a dream, a cloud giving shade, from which butter and honey were dropping, and I saw people collecting it in their hands; some gathering much and some little. And behold, there was a rope extending from the earth to the sky, and I saw that you (the Prophet ﷺ) grasped it and ascended, then another man grasped it and ascended, and (after that) another (third) grasped it and ascended, but then when another (fourth) man held it, it broke yet was then re-connected.' Abu Bakr said, 'O Allah's Messenger! Let my father be sacrificed for you! Allow me to interpret this dream.' The

---
[85] Al-Baghawi's *'Sharh as-Sunnah'*: 12/237.
[86] *"Fat'h al-Bari"*: 12/400.

Prophet ﷺ said to him, 'Interpret it.' Abu Bakr ؓ said, 'The cloud with shade symbolizes Islam, and the butter and honey, dropping from it, symbolize the Qur'an; its sweetness descending, as some people will learn much of the Qur'an and others a little. The rope, which was extended from the sky to the earth, is the Truth, which you (the Prophet) are following. You follow it, so Allah will raise you high with it, and then another man would follow it and would rise up with it, and then another person would follow it, and then another man would try to follow it, yet it would break but would then be reconnected for him, so that he would also rise up with it. O Allah's Messenger! Let my father be sacrificed for you! Am I right or wrong?' The Prophet ﷺ replied, 'You are right in part of it, but wrong in another part." Abu Bakr ؓ said, 'O Allah's Prophet! By Allah, you must tell me in what part I was wrong." The Prophet ﷺ said, 'Do not swear.'"[87]

Al-Baghawi said: "Dreaming of clouds is interpreted as wisdom. Therefore, dreaming of mounting on top of clouds, without fear, may be interpreted as being very wise. However, if one dreams that the clouds are black or windy, it may be interpreted as a punishment. If the clouds carry rain, it is a sign of mercy. On the other hand, honey and butter may also be interpreted as wealth, in a dream.

---

[87] Sahih al-Bukhari: 12/431, Sahih Muslim: 15/28-29, at-Tirmidhi: 9/159, Ibn Majah: Hadith No. 3918 and al-Baghawi in "*Sharh as-Sunnah*": 12/216-217.

It is reported that a man asked Ibn Sireen: "I dreamed last night as if I was licking honey from a bowl made of gemstone." Ibn Sireen said to him: "Fear Allah and try to recite the Qur'an again, for you are a man who has memorized the Qur'an but has forgotten it."[88]

An-Nawawi said: "As for the Prophet's statement to Abu Bakr ؒ: **"You are right in some of it and wrong in some"**, the scholars have different opinions with regards to its meaning. Ibn Qutaibah and others have said: "It means that Abu Bakr was right in interpreting its meaning but wrong in starting explaining it without the Prophet's consent." Others, however, have said: "What Ibn Qutaibah and others have said is wrong because the Prophet ﷺ allowed Abu Bakr ؒ to interpret it, saying: "Interpret it." However, Abu Bakr ؒ was wrong in not interpreting the whole dream. The man said: **"I saw in a dream, a cloud giving shade. Butter and honey** were dropping from it" and Abu Bakr ؒ interpreted both honey and butter as the Qur'an, whereas he ؒ should have interpreted **honey as the Qur'an** and **butter as the Sunnah**. At-Tahhawi has interpreted them as the Qur'an and Sunnah."[89]

---

[88] *"Sharh as-Sunnah"*: 12/220.
[89] *"Sharh an-Nawawi ala' Sahih Muslim"*: 15/29.

## A Green Garden

Dreaming of a green garden may be interpreted as Islam; others have said that it may indicate religious books. Qais Ibn Ubadah ؓ has said: "I was sitting in a gathering in which there was Sa'd Ibn Malik and Ibn Omar. Abdullah Ibn Sallaam passed in front of them, so they said, 'This man is from the people of Paradise.' I said to Abdullah Ibn Sallaam, 'They said so-and-so.' He replied, '*Subhan Allah*! They ought not to have said things of which they have no knowledge, but I saw (in a dream) that a post was fixed in a green garden. At the top of the post there was a handhold and below it there was a servant. I was asked to climb (the post). So I climbed it till I took hold of the handhold.' Then I narrated this dream to Allah's Messenger ﷺ. Allah's Messenger ﷺ said:[90] 'Abdullah will die while still holding on to the firm reliable handhold (i.e., Islam).'"

## Scales

Dreaming of scales (a balance) may be interpreted as a sign of justice.

Abu Bakrah ؓ reported: "One day the Prophet ﷺ said: 'Which of you had dream?' A man said: 'It was I. I saw as though a pair of scales descend from the sky. You and Abu Bakr were weighed and you were heavier; Abu Bakr

---

[90] Sahih al-Bukhari: 12/397, Sahih Muslim: 16/42-43 and al-Baghari's '*Sharh as-Sunnah*': 12/230.

and Omar were weighed and Abu Bakr was heavier. Omar and Uthman were weighed and Omar was heavier; then the scale was taken up. We saw the signs of dislike on the face of the Messenger of Allah ﷺ."[91]

Ibn al-Arabi, may Allah have Mercy upon him, said: "With regards to the interpretation of the Hadith of the Scales, Allah ﷻ has said,
❨and the heaven He has raised high, and He has set up the Balance❩ (55: 7).
Our scholars have stated that **the Balance** in the above Verse refers to **the Balance of Justice**. People should act justly to one other and observe due balance in all their actions. Balancing two well-known things shows justice. The Prophet ﷺ and Abu Bakr ؓ were weighed, and the Prophet ﷺ was heavier (with regard to their virtues and deeds). Abu Bakr ؓ and Omar Ibn al-Khattab ؓ were weighed, and Abu Bakr ؓ was heavier. Omar ؓ and Uthman ؓ were weighed, and Omar ؓ was heavier. The scale was then lifted, which indicates that there is no one left who might deserve to be compared with them." [92]

Interpreting dreams from a Hadith's perspective also includes the examples, which the Prophet ﷺ has given. He ﷺ has quoted, as an example, a believer for a palm tree, and described travelling as torture. He ﷺ said: "Travelling is a kind of torture, as it prevents one from

---

[91] At-Tirmidhi: 9/149-150 and classified as *Hasan Sahih*. Albani classified it as *Sahih* (1864).
[92] "*A'rida al-Ahudit*": 9/137-138.

eating, drinking and sleeping properly. So, when one's needs are fulfilled, one should return quickly to one's family."[93]

There are so many similar examples, which are difficult to examine thoroughly.

## C- Interpreting Dreams from the Meaning of Names

Al-Baghawi said: "Interpreting dreams by their words means: If one dreams of a man named Raashid (meaning: rightly guided), it is interpreted as Rushd (guidance); if he is called Saalim (in Arabic it means: Secure), it is interpreted as Salamah (Security)."[94]

Anas Ibn Malik ؓ reported that the Prophet ﷺ said: "I saw, last night in my dream, as if we were in the house of Uqbah Ibn Rafi'. The fresh dates of Ibn Tab were brought to us. I interpreted this as sublimity for us in this world, and a good ending in the Hereafter, and that our religion was good."[95]

The word **Tab** is derived from the Arabic language, meaning: Good, pleasant, to be or become delicious and

---

[93] Sahih al-Bukhari: 3/622, Sahih Muslim: 13/70 and Imam Malik: 2/980.
[94] *"Sharh as-Sunnah"*: 12/222.
[95] Sahih Muslim: 15/30-31 and al-Baghawi's *"Sharh as-Sunnah"*: 12/222.

delightful. An-Nawawi said: "Ibn Tab was a man who used to live in Madinah, and the Prophet's statement: **"our religion is good"** means, it is complete, as its rules and foundations have been established." [96]

Salim Ibn Abdillah Ibn Omar ؓ reported that the Prophet ﷺ said: "I saw (in a dream) a black woman with unkempt hair leaving of Madinah and settling at Mahai'ah, (i.e., Al-Juhfah). I interpreted that as a symbol of an epidemic in Madinah being transferred to that place (Al-Juhfah)."[97]

Al-Muhallab said: "From the word **'Black'** one derives epidemic and disease, and from **'unkempt hair'** one derives the mess and chaos which will emerge from Madinah."[98]

Some have stated that dreaming of saying goodbye (farewell) to someone is good, because it indicates: remarriage with one's divorced wife, settlement of a dispute with one's partner, profit for a businessman, return of one's position in government, and recovery from an illness. The word *'Tawdi'* (farewell) in Arabic is derived from the words *'Da'a'* meaning: composure and relaxation..

---

[96] *"Sharh an-Nawawi ala' Sahih Muslim"*: 15/31.
[97] Sahih al-Bukhari: 12/425, at-Tirmidhi: 9/147-148 and Ibn Majah: Hadith No. 3924.
[98] *"Fat'h al-Bari"*: 12/426.

## A Knot

Someone has said: I hate dreaming of a knot, or fastening something with a knot, but I like dreaming about unfastening a knot, because knots symbolise grief and depression and unfastening them symbolises freedom from grief or sorrow, release from suffering; being joyful and a happy ending.

## A Voice

Dreaming of a voice is interpreted as a man's good reputation and standing. Therefore, whoever dreams that his voice is strong, it is indicated that he would have a good reputation among people, but if his voice is weak, it would be the opposite.

## Marriage, Eyesight, Peace and Charity

Whoever dreams that he has married a short, black woman, it is indicated by her colour of her wealth, and her shortness of her short life. Eyesight in a dream indicates understanding of religion, peace indicates security, and *Sadaqah* (charity) is interpreted as truthfulness, because it derives from the word *Sidq* (truthfulness).

## Remembrance of Allah and Gold

Dreaming of making *Dhikr* (remembrance of Allah) indicates that one has a good reputation among people, and *Dhahab* (gold) denotes one's bad interpretation because it is derived from the word *'Adh-Dhahaab'*, meaning: departure, and its yellow colour is interpreted as sadness and grief.

## Europeans

Dreaming of *Firanjah* (Europeans) is interpreted as support and relief because the word *Faraj* (relief and support) is derived from *Asnaan*.

## Christians

Dreaming of a *Nasrani* (Christian) indicates that one will be triumphant over his opponent, because the word *'Nasrani'*, which is derived from the word *'Nusra'* which in Arabic, means: support and assistance.

## Jews

Dreaming of a *Yahudi* (Jew) indicates that Allah's Mercy will be bestowed upon someone, because the word *Yahud* in Arabic means *Yatub*, that is, to repent and be guided.

## Beds

Dreaming of *Asirra* (plural of *Sarir*), meaning beds in Arabic, is interpreted as happiness, because it is derived from the word '*Surur*', that is, happiness and joy. Therefore, dreaming of an unknown bed is good. If one dreams that one is sitting on it, it indicates that one will become a ruler or achieve a high position; if one is single, one will get married, and if a woman is pregnant she will have a baby boy.

## Sheep

Dreaming of *Ghanam* (sheep) is interpreted as spoils and booty because the word *Ghanimah* (spoils) in Arabic is derived from the word *Ghanam*.

## The Head

Dreaming of *Ar-Ra's* (the head) is interpreted as becoming a leader or ruler, because the word *Ra'is* (leader, chief, boss, etc) is derived from the word *Ar-Ra's*.

## Teeth

Whoever dreams that all his *Asnaan* (teeth) have fallen out, it is indicated that people of his age will die before him, because the word *Sinn* (similar age in Arabic) derives from the word *Asnaan*.

## Surat Al-Fatihah

Whoever dreams that he is reading *Surat Al-Fatihah*, it is interpreted that Allah ﷻ will bestow His Bounties upon him.

## A Key

Dreaming of a key (*Mifta'h* in Arabic) may be interpreted as a sign of livelihood, the blessings of Allah, support, wealth, fortune, etc. because it is derived from the verb *Fataha* (to open). It can also be interpreted as acquiring knowledge or memorizing the Qur'an. If high dignitaries and kings dream of keys, it indicates that they will conquer new lands. *Mifta'h* can indicate help and victory, as Allah ﷻ has said,
❰help from Allah and a near victory (*Fat'h*)❱ (61: 13).

## A Necklace

Dreaming of a necklace (*Qilaadah* in Arabic) is interpreted in many respects. Whoever dreams that he/she is wearing a necklace, it is indicated that he/she will be appointed to an office, because the word *Qilaada* is derived from the verb *Taqallada* in Arabic, meaning: be appointed to or be in charge of a high position. The better and more valuable the necklace is, the higher the position is.

## Becoming a Monk

Some interpreters of dreams have said: Whoever is pious and dreams of becoming a *Raahib* (monk), it indicates that he fears Allah ﷻ much, because the word *Raahib* is derived from the verb *Rahiba* in Arabic, that is, to fear. Allah ﷻ says,
❮**draw your hand close to your side (to guard) against *Rahb* (i.e., fear)**❯ (28: 32).

## Names

Others have stated that if one dreams of a name related to Allah ﷻ, such as Abdullah or Abdurrahman, it is interpreted as Allah's care and support for him. If it is another name such as Muhammad, Yunus etc, it has two interpretations: If the name is related to someone who is pious and a devout Muslim, it is a glad tiding; however, if it is related to someone evil and corrupt, it is a warning and threat.

# D. Interpreting Dreams from the Meaning of the Proverb

Al-Baghawi, may Allah have Mercy upon him, said: "Dreams can also be interpreted by proverbs, such as: dreaming of a jeweler is interpreted as a liar, because people say: 'the worst liars are jewelers' (Arabic proverb), and digging a hole is interpreted as deception and cunning, because people say: 'to dig one's own grave', and Allah ﷻ says,
⟨**and the evil plot encompasses but the men who make it**⟩ (36: 43).

## A Long Hand

Dreaming of a long hand is interpreted as doing favours to other people, because they say: 'to lend a helping hand', and dreaming of throwing stones or arches (*Ramy* in Arabic) is interpreted as defamation and false accusation of fornication; Allah ﷻ says,
⟨**and those who *Yarmuna* (i.e., accuse) chaste women**⟩ (24: 6).

## Washing Hands

Dreaming of washing one's hands is interpreted as hopelessness, because people say: 'I wash my hands of you.'"[99]

## A Pair of Scissors

Some interpreters of dreams have stated: Dreaming of a pair of scissors may be interpreted as someone who severs relations, and a needle may be interpreted as someone who unites people.

# E. Interpreting Dreams by their Meaning

## A Citrus Fruit

Abu Sai'd al-Wa'idh said: "Whoever dreams that he is cutting a citrus fruit will be praised and admired, because the Prophet ﷺ said: "The example of a believer who recites the Qur'an and acts on it, is like a citron (a citrus fruit) which tastes and smells nice." Others, though, have stated that this indicates hypocrisy, for those who are not religious, devoted or pious, because its outer appearance does not reflect what is inside.

---

[99] "*Sharh as-Sunnah*": 12/222.

## Flowers

Al-Baghawi said: "Dreaming of flowers and narcissus (daffodil) may be interpreted as a sign of short stay because they do not last long, and dreaming of myrtle (an evergreen shrub with shiny leaves and sweet-smelling white flowers) may be interpreted as a long stay, because it lasts longer. It is reported that a woman asked an interpreter of dreams, in a place called Ahwaaz, by saying: 'I have seen, in my dream, that as if my husband has given me a narcissus and gave his other wife a myrtle.' He replied: 'Your husband will divorce you, but keep his other wife.[100]

## F. Interpreting Dreams by their Opposite Meaning

Dreams can be interpreted by their opposite meaning. For example: dreaming of fear may be interpreted as security and safety, as Allah ﷻ has said,

❮and He will surely give them, in exchange, a safe security, after their fear❯ (24: 55)

and vice versa, so dreaming of security is interpreted as fear. Dreaming of crying is interpreted as happiness, laughter as sadness, as Allah ﷻ has said,

❮Let them laugh a little: much will they weep❯ (9: 82);

---

[100] *"Sharh as-Sunnah"*: 12/223.

a plague is interpreted as war and vice versa; love as madness and vice versa; and dreaming of thirst is better than dreaming of water and irrigation. Likewise, dreaming of poverty is interpreted as richness and vice versa, and dreaming of being wounded and hit is better than dreaming of wounding or hitting someone.[101]

---

[101] *"Sharh as-Sunnah"*: 12/224.

# Rules and Benefits Concering Dreams

**1-** A good dream is not a source of judgement nor laying of Islamic rules. If anyone dreams that someone is ordering him to commit an evil act, which contradicts Islamic teachings and claims that it is from Allah ﷻ or from His Prophet ﷺ, he is not allowed to do what he was ordered to in his dream, because Allah ﷻ has already completed His Religion (Islam),
❲**This day I have perfected your religion for you completed my favour upon you and have chosen for you Islam as your Religion**❳ (5: 3).

Some scholars, among them Abu Ishaaq al-Asfara'ini, have stated that if anyone dreams of the Prophet ﷺ who orders him to do something, he should do it. However, the majority of scholars have refused this opinion and confirmed that any dream that disagrees with *Shari'ah* should be rejected, but if it happens to agree with it, it is an indication that should in fact be taken into consideration. If it neither agrees with it nor disagrees, it is then permissible to act upon it. The following are some of the statements made by some notable scholars:

An-Nawawi, may Allah have Mercy upon him, said: "Although a dream may come true, it should not be used as an Islamic judgement, because the state of being asleep is not a state for acquiring accuracy and precision in what the dreamer hears. It is unanimously agreed among Muslim scholars that one of the conditions of accepting someone's testimony or narration is to be awake, speaking accurately and flawlessly. But a sleeping person does not have these abilities."[102]

Ibn al-Haaj, may Allah have Mercy upon him, said: "Allah ﷻ does not order His Servants to do what they see in their dreams, because the Prophet ﷺ said: 'There are three (persons) whose actions are not recorded: **a sleeper till he awakes**, a boy till he reaches puberty, and a lunatic till he comes to reason.'[103] Therefore, a sleeper is not ordered to do what he sees in his dreams."[104]

**2-** A good dream is divided into two aspects: One is clear and easily interpreted, and one concealed with hidden content. Al-Baghawi said: "One may have his dream come true, such as dreaming of Hajj, a fortune or a misfortune. The Prophet ﷺ dreamed about the conquest of Makkah and it was fulfilled; Allah ﷻ says,
❨**Indeed Allah shall fulfil the true vision which He showed to His Messenger, in very truth**❩ (48: 27)[105],

---

[102] From a book called "*Min Af'al ar-rasul'*" by al-Ashqar: 2/162.
[103] Reported by Abu Dawud, on the authority of Ali Ibn Abi Ta'lib ؓ

[104] From a book called "*Min Af'al ar-rasul*'" by al-Ashqar: 2/162.
[105] In his dream, the Prophet ﷺ saw that he has entered Makkah along with his Companions, with their (heads) hair having been shaved and cut short.

and one may also have a dream concealed with hidden content, that requires wisdom and knowledge to interpret.[106]

**3-** An-Nabulsi has said: "You should know that a single dream may have different interpretations, according to the language and country of the people. For example: *Safarjal* (quince: hard yellowish pear-shaped fruit) is interpreted as beauty, pride and relaxation for the Persian people, but for the Arabs it is interpreted as travel and departure because it is derived from the word *Safar* in Arabic, meaning travelling and *Jala'* meaning departure and emigration. A dream can also have different interpretations, due to the religion of the people. For example, dreaming of eating *Maitah* (meat of an animal not slaughtered in accordance with the Islamic rituals) is interpreted as earning illegal money or as a misfortune, according to the people who believe that eating *Maita* is unlawful (*Haraam*), but it is interpreted as a benefit and fortune according to those who consider it to be lawful.

A dream can also be interpreted differently according to the different seasons. For example, dreaming of hot water, hot weather, sunshine or warm clothes is interpreted as a relief and relaxation, for those who have caught a severe cold and live in the cold, but is interpreted as a disease and misfortune in summer time.

---

[106] "*Sharh as-Sunnah*": 12/224--225.

In general, people's culture and religions should be taken into consideration when interpreting dreams."[107]

**4-** Al-Baghawi said: "Interpreting a dream could be changed by adding or deleting. For example: dreaming of crying is interpreted as happiness, but if accompanied by a sound, it is interpreted as a disaster. Dreaming of laughter is interpreted as sadness and sorrow, but if it comes with a smile it is interpreted as good. A similar dream could change from one person to another. For example, Ibn Sireen interpreted the dream of someone who dreamt of giving a *Khutbah* (sermon) as a sign of achieving high status, but if he was not qualified for that position, Ibn Sireen interpreted the same dream as a sign of being crucified. A man asked Ibn Sireen: 'I have seen in my dream as if I am making *Adhan*.' Ibn Sireen interpreted it, saying: 'You will perform the pilgrimage.' Another man asked him about the same dream (*Adhan*), and he said: 'Your hand will be cut off.' When he was asked about it, Ibn Sireen said: 'I saw that the first person had good characteristics and I interpreted it with Allah's Verse,

❲and make *Adhan* (proclaim) to mankind the Hajj❳ (22: 27),

but I did not like the second one's appearance and so I interpreted it with Allah's Verse,

❲then shouted a crier: "O you in the caravan" Surely you are thieves!"❳ (12: 70)."[108]

---

[107] "*Ta'teer al-Anaam*": 2/359-361.
[108] "*Sharh as-Sunnah*": 12/224.

Al-Baghawi added: "One might see, in a dream, a particular person, but it could be interpreted in favour of his son or relative; the Prophet ﷺ saw, in a dream, that Abu Jahl had pledged his allegiance to him, but it turned out to be that his son, Ikrimah ؓ, was the one who had pledged his allegiance to the Prophet ﷺ. When Ikrimah embraced Islam, the Prophet ﷺ said: "That is it."[109] The Prophet ﷺ also saw in a dream that Usaid Ibn al-A's would be governor of Makkah, but it turned out that his son, Attab Ibn Usaid, was appointed as governor of Makka; the Prophet ﷺ himself appointed him.'

---

[109] *"Sharh as-Sunnah"*: 12/

# Some Rare Interpretations of our Ancestors

This section will deal with some interpretations of famous interpreters, so that the reader may practise interpreting dreams after acquiring the necessary knowledge and tools.

- It is reported that Omar Ibn Al-Khattab ﷺ appointed someone as judge of Shaam (Syria, Lebanon and Palestine). On his way to Shaam, the judge saw, in a dream, as if the moon and the sun were fighting and the stars are fighting, some on the moon's side and some on the sun's side, and the judge was a star. He returned to Omar ﷺ to inform him about his dream. Omar ﷺ asked him: 'Why did you return?' The judge narrated what he had seen in the dream. Omar ﷺ asked him: 'When you saw yourself as a star, on which side were you; with the moon or the sun?' The judge said: 'With the moon.' Omar Ibn al-Khattab ﷺ said: 'You are dismissed from your position as judge.' When the man left, Omar ﷺ said to his companions, 'If his dream comes true, he will be one of the people who will revolt against us.' At the battle of Siffin, this man was killed fighting alongside the army of Shaam.[110]

- A woman came to Ibn Sireen and said: "I have seen, in a dream, two pearls in my room, one was greater than the other. My sister asked me to give her one and I gave her the little one." Ibn Sireen replied: "If your dream is true, it means you have learnt two Surahs of the Qur'an, one is longer than the other and you have taught your sister the shortest one." She replied: "Yes".

- A woman came to Ibn Sireen and said: "I have seen, in a dream, that the threshold of my upper door has fallen on the bottom one, and the two leaves of the door have fallen out, one outside the house and one inside." Ibn Sireen replied: "Do you have a husband and two sons who are away?" She replied: "Yes". He said: "As for the threshold, it means that your husband will be coming home soon, and for the leaf that fell outside of the house, it means that your son will marry a strange woman." Soon afterwards, her husband returned home, and her son brought home a strange unknown wife.

- A man came to Ibn Abbas ؓ and said: "I have seen, in a dream, as if I was lowering a bucket in a well, and two thirds of the bucket became full." Ibn Abbas ؓ replied:

---

[110] To interpret the judge's dream, Omar Ibn al-Khattab ؓ used as proof Allah's verse, ❮We have made the Night and the Day as two (of Our) Signs: the Sign of the Night have We obscured while the Sign of the day We have made to enlighten you❯ (17: 12).

"You have been away from your wife for six months and your wife is pregnant and she will give birth to a baby boy." The man asked: "What is your proof?" Ibn Abbas said: "I have interpreted the well as a woman; the glad tiding in the well was Yusuf ﷺ; that is how I knew your wife would give birth to a boy. As for two the thirds of the bucket, it indicates that she has been pregnant for six months." The man said: "You are right, I have just received a letter from my wife and she is six months pregnant now."

- A man came to Ibn Sireen and said: 'I have seen in a dream as if I am sleeping with my mother and my sister.' Ibn Sireen could not tell the man in person, so he wrote to him saying, 'This person is disobedient to his mother, severs the bonds of kinship, ungrateful and insults his mother and sister.'

- A man came to Ibn Sireen and said: "I have seen, in a dream, as if a man is standing in the middle of a mosque, that is the mosque of al-Basrah, holding a sword in his hand and breaking a rock." Ibn Sireen replied: "This man should be al-Hasan al-Basri." The man said: "I swear by Allah that it is al-Hasan al-Basri." Ibn Sireen then said: "I interpreted 'standing in the middle of a mosque' as someone who devoted himself to Islam and ' the sword breaking the rock', as telling the truth with regards to religion."

- Ibn Sireen was asked about a man who saw himself, in a dream, as if wearing a new Yemeni garment, but which was torn at edges. He replied: "This man has memorized and learnt some of the Qur'an but then forgotten it.'

- A man came to Ibn Sireen and said: "I have dreamt as if I was drawing water, then took a glass of water and put it on my hand, but the glass broke and the water remained on my hand." Ibn Sireen replied: "Do you have a wife?" The man said: "Yes". Ibn Sireen asked: "Is she pregnant?" The man said: "Yes". Ibn Sireen said: "She will give birth and then die, but the child will live."

- A man came to Ibn Sireen and said: "I have seen, in a dream, that my thigh is red and hair grows on it, and I ordered a man to cut that hair off." Ibn Sireen replied: "You are a man indebted and a man from your relatives will pay it off, on your behalf."

- It is reported that Harun ar-Rashid saw, in a dream, that the Angel of Death came to him, so he asked him: "O Angel of Death, how long will I live?" The Angel pointed out to him with his five fingers, and Harun ar-Rashid woke up furious and weeping. He narrated it to a famous interpreter who said: "O Commander of the Believers, the Angel of Death has informed you about five things whose knowledge are with Allah Alone, and the following verse includes them,
**《Verily the knowledge of the Hour is with Allah (alone). It is He Who sends down rain and He Who**

knows what is in the wombs. Nor does anyone know what it is that he will earn on the morrow: nor does anyone know in what land he is to die. Verily with Allah is Full Knowledge and He is Acquainted (with all things)⟩ (31: 34).

Harun ar-Rashid smiled and felt happy.

- A man came to Ibn Sireen and said: "I have seen, in a dream, as if I am drinking from a narrow jug." Ibn Sireen said: "you are trying to seduce a woman-slave against her will."

- A woman came to an interpreter and said: "I have seen, in a dream, as if I had a basin made of pure gold but it was broken, I threw myself to the ground, trying to look for it, but I could not find it." The interpreter asked her: "Do you have a sick servant?" She said: "Yes". He said: "He will die."

- A man came to Ibn Sireen and said: "I have seen, in a dream, as if a snake was moving quickly and I was following it. It entered a hole and I put a shovel on top of the hole." Ibn Sireen asked the man: "Are you intending to marry any woman?" The man said: "Yes." Ibn Sireen said: "You will marry her and inherit from her." The man later married the woman who left him seven thousands Dirham after her death.

- It is reported that a man came to Ibn Sireen and said: "I have seen, in a dream, as if I am riding an elephant." Ibn

Sireen said: "Elephants are not part of Muslims' means of transport. I am afraid that you are on a religion other than Islam."

- A woman came to Ibn Sireen and said: "I have seen, in a dream, as if I killed my husband with some people." Ibn Sireen replied: "You have forced your husband to commit a sin, so fear Allah." The woman said: "You are right."

# *Glossary*

**Allah ta'Ala:** Allah, the Most High, the Lord of all the worlds. Allah, the supreme and mighty Name, indicates the One, the Existent, the Creator, the Worshipped, the Lord of the Universe. Allah is the First without beginning and the Last without end and the Outwardly Manifest and the Inwardly Hidden.

**ahlu'l-sunnah wa'l-jama'a:** the people who follow the sunnah of the Prophet Muhammad, may Allah bless him and grant him peace, and who hold together as a community on that basis.

**'alim:** a man of knowledge from amongst the Muslims who acts on what he knows

**'aqeedah:** belief or faith firmly based on how things are, rather than on how they may be imagined. Thus 'aqeedah can only fully be derived from an original revelation from Allah and from the sayings of the Messenger to whom it was revealed: in this age, the Qur'an and the Prophet Muhammad, may Allah bless him and grant him peace

**ayah:** a sign, a verse of the Qur'an.

**ayat:** the plural of ayah.

**bara':** withdrawing from and opposing all that is displeasing to Allah and His Messenger, may Allah bless him and grant him peace.

**bid'a:** innovation, changing the original teaching of the Prophet Muhammad, may Allah bless him and grant him peace.

**deen:** the life-transaction, submission and obedience to a particular system of rules and practices, a debt of exchange between two parties, in this usage between the Creator and the created. Allah says in the Qur'an: Surely the deen with Allah is Islam. (3.19).

**faqih:** a scholar of fiqh who by virtue of his knowledge can give an authoritative opinion or judgement.

**fiqh:** Islamic jurisprudence, the science of the application of the sharia

**fisq:** corruption.

**fuqaha:** the plural of faqih.

**hadith:** reported speech, particularly of, or about, the Prophet Muhammad, may Allah bless him and grant him peace.

**hadith qudsi:** those words of Allah on the tongue of His Prophet, may Allah bless him and grant him peace, which are not part of the Revelation of the Qur'an

**hajj:** the annual pilgrimage to Makka which every Muslim who has the means and ability must make once in his or her life-time; the performance of the rites of the hajj in the protected area which surrounds the Ka'aba. The hajj is one of the indispensable pillars of Islam.

**halal:** permitted by the shari'ah.

**haram:** forbidden by the shari'ah; also a protected area, an inviolable place or object

**hasan:** good; a category of hadith which is reliable, but which is not as well authenticated as one which is sahih.

**hijrah:** emigration in the way of Allah. Islam takes its dating from the hijrah of the Prophet Muhammad, may Allah bless him and grant him peace, from Makka to Madina, in 622 A.

**ihsan:** the state of being hasan; being absolutely sincere to Allah in oneself; it is to worship Allah as though you see Him, knowing that although you do not see Him, He sees you.

**imam:** the one who leads the prayer, an eminent scholar.

**iman:** acceptance, belief, trust, in Allah, a gift from Him. Iman is to believe in Allah, His angels, His revealed Books, His messengers, the Last Day, the Garden and the Fire, and that everything is by the Decree of Allah, both the good and the evil.

**Islam:** peace and submission to the will of Allah, the way of life embodied by all the prophets, given its final form in the prophetic guidance brought by the Prophet Muhammad, may the blessings and peace of Allah be on him. The five pillars of Islam are the affirmation of the shahada, doing the salat, paying the zakat, fasting the month of Ramadan, and doing the hajj once in a life-time if you are able.

**isnad:** the written record of the names of the people who form the chain of human transmission, person to person, by means of which a hadith is preserved.
One of the sciences of the Muslims which was developed after the Prophet Muhammad's death, may Allah bless him and grant him peace, is the science of assessing the authenticity of a hadith by assessing the reliability of its isnad.

**jahiliyyah:** the time of ignorance, before the coming of Islam.

**jihad:** struggle, particularly warfare, to establish and defend Islam. Inwardly, the jihad is to oppose whatever in your self is displeasing to Allah. Outwardly, it is oppose kufr by word and action.

**jinn:** unseen beings created from smokeless fire who co-habit the earth together with mankind

**Ka'aba:** the cube-shaped building at the centre of the Haram in Makka, originally built by the Prophet Ibrahim, peace be on him, and rebuilt with the help of the Prophet Muhammad, may Allah bless him and grant him peace; also known as the House of Allah. The Ka'aba is the focal point which all Muslims face when doing the salat. This does not mean that Allah lives inside the Ka'aba, nor does it mean that the Muslims worship the Ka'aba. It is Allah Who is worshipped and Allah is not contained or confined in any form or place or time or concept.

**kafir:** a person who commits kufr, the opposite of a mumin.

**kafirun:** the plural of kafir.

**kalima:** the declaration: There is no god but Allah, Muhammad is the Messenger of Allah

**kufr:** to cover up the truth, to reject Allah and His Messenger, may the blessings and peace of Allah be on him.

**la ilaha illa'llah:** there is no god but Allah.

**makruh:** disapproved of, without being forbidden, by the shari'ah.

**marfu':** a hadith from a companion of the Prophet Muhammad containing words attributed to the Prophet Muhammad, may Allah bless him and grant him peace.

**Muhammad ar-Rasulu'llah:** Muhammad is the Messenger of Allah, may the blessings and peace of Allah be on h

**muhsin:** someone who possesses the quality of ihsan, who remembers Allah constantly.

**mumin:** someone who possesses the quality of iman, who trusts in Allah and accepts His Messenger, may Allah bless him and grant him peace.

**muminun:** the plural of mumin.

**munafiq:** a hypocrite; the hypocrites amongst the Muslims outwardly profess Islam on the tongue, but inwardly reject Allah and His Messenger, may Allah bless him and grant him peace, siding with the kafirun against the Muslims. The deepest part of the Fire is reserved for the munafiqun

**munafiqun:** the plural of munafiq.

**mushrik:** one who commits shirk.

**mushrikeen:** the plural of mushrik.

**muslim:** someone who follows the way of Islam, doing what is obligatory, avoiding what is forbidden, keeping within the limits prescribed by Allah, and following the sunnah of the Prophet Muhammad, may Allah bless him and grant him peace, in what he or she is able. A Muslim is, by definition, one who is safe and sound, at peace in this world, and promised the Garden in the next world.

**nifaq:** hypocrisy.

**qadi:** a judge.

**qiblah:** the direction faced in prayer, which, for the Muslims, is towards the Ka'aba in Makka. Everyone has a direction in life, but only the Muslims have this qibla

**Qur'an:** the 'Recitation', the last Revelation from Allah to mankind and the jinn before the end of the world, revealed to the Prophet Muhammad, may Allah bless him and grant him peace, through the angel Jibril, over a period of twenty-three years, the first thirteen of which were spent in Makka and the last ten of which were spent in Madina. The Qur'an amends, encompasses, expands, surpasses and abrogates all the earlier revelations revealed to the earlier messengers, peace be on all of them. The Qur'an is the greatest miracle given to the

Prophet Muhammad by Allah, for he was illiterate and could neither read nor write. The Qur'an is the uncreated word of Allah. The Qur'an still exists today exactly as it was originally revealed, without any alteration or change or addition or deletion. Whoever recites the Qur'an with courtesy and sincerity receives knowledge and wisdom, for it is the well of wisdom in this age.

**rak'a:** a unit of the prayer, a complete series of standing, bowing, prostrations and sitti
**rak'at:** the plural of rak'a.

**Ramadan:** the month of fasting, the ninth month in the Muslim lunar calendar, during which all adult Muslims who are in good health fast from the first light of dawn until sunset each day. The Qur'an was first revealed in the month of Ramadan. The fast of Ramadan is one of the indispensable pillars of Islam.

**sahaba:** companions, particularly the com-panions of the Prophet Muhammad, may the blessings and peace of Allah be on him and on his family and on his companion

**sahih:** healthy and sound with no defects; often used to describe a fully authenticated hadith. The two most reliable collections of hadith by Imam Al-Bukhari and Imam Muslim are both described as sahih.

**salafi:** adjective from as-salaf, 'the early years', and used generally to describe the early generations of the

Muslims, particularly the sahaba, the companions of the Messenger of Allah, may the blessings and peace of Allah be on him and on his family and on his companions. In the present age the term is sometimes used to describe those Muslims who closely follow the sunnah of the Prophet Muhammad.

**salat:** the prayer, particularly the five daily obligatory ritual prayers of the Muslims which are called maghrib, 'isha, fajr, dhur and 'asr. They consist of fixed numbers of rak'at in worship to Allah. Salat is one of the indispensable pillars

**sawm:** fasting, particularly the fast of Ramadan, from food and drink and making love if you are married during daylight, from the first light of dawn until sunset.

**shahada:** to witness, to bear witness that: There is no god but Allah and that Muhammad is the Messenger of Allah, may Allah bless him and grant him peace. The shahada is the gateway to Islam and the gateway to the Garden in the next world. It is easy to say, but to act on it is a vast undertaking which has far-reaching conse-quences, both in inward awareness and in outward action, both in this world and in the next world. Continual affirmation of the shahada is one of the indispensable pillars of Islam.

**shari'ah:** a road, the legal and social modality of a people based on the revelation of their prophet. The last shari'ah in history is that of Islam. It abrogates all previous shari'ahs. It is, being the last, therefore the easiest to follow, for it is applicable to the whole human race wherever they are.

**shaytan:** a devil, particularly Iblis (Satan), an evil jinn who prompts mankind and the jinn to rebel against Allah. Shaytan is part of the creation of Allah, and we seek refuge in Allah from the evil that He has created

**shirk:** the unforgiveable wrong action of worshipping something or someone other than Allah or associating something or someone as a partner with Him; the opposite of Tawheed which is affirmation of Divine Unity. Shirk is idol-worship, which is attributing form to Allah by attempting to confine Him within an object, a concept, a ritual or a myth whereas Allah is not like anything and has no form. He cannot be conceived of or perceived.

**sirah:** the historical study of the Prophet Muhammad's life, may the blessings and peace of Allah be on

**sunnah:** a form, the customary practice of a person or group of people. It has come to refer almost exclusively to the practice of the Messenger of Allah, Muhammad, may Allah bless him and grant him peace, but also comprises the customs of the first generation of Muslims in Madina, who acted in accordance with what they had learned from him and who transmitted what they had learned to the next generation. The sunnah is a complete behavioural science that has been systematically kept outside the learning framework of this society, but which nevertheless has been preserved by those to whom it has been transmitted and who continue to embody it as their way of life. The Messenger of Allah, may Allah bless him and grant him peace, said: 'I have left two matters with you. As long as you hold to them, you will not go the wrong way. They are the Book of Allah and the Sunnah of His Prophet.' (Al-Muwatta of Imam Malik, 46.1.3)

**tafsir:** commentary on the Qur'an.

**taqwa:** being careful, knowing your place in the cosmos. Its proof is the experience of awe of Allah, which inspires a person to be on guard against wrong action and eager for actions which are pleasing to Him.

**tawaf:** circling the Ka'aba; tawaf is done in sets of seven circuits followed by two rak'at of prayer

**tawba:** returning to correct action after error, turning away from wrong action to Allah and asking His Forgiveness, turning to face the Reality whereas before one turned one's back

**Tawheed:** the Divine Unity, Unity in its most profound sense. Allah is One in His Essence and His Attributes and

His Acts. The whole of the creation and what it contains is one unified event which in itself has no lasting reality. Allah is the Real: Surely we come from Allah and surely to Him we return. (2.156

**'ulama:** the plural of 'alim.

**Ummah:** the body of the Muslims as one distinct and integrated community or nation.

**wala':** loyalty, holding fast to all that is pleasing to Allah and His Messenger, may Allah bless him and grant him peace. Whoever possesses al-wala' wa'l-bara' loves with the love of Allah and hates with the hate of Allah

**zakat:** the wealth tax obligatory on Muslims each year, usually payable in the form of one fortieth of surplus wealth which is more than a certain fixed minimum amount, which is called the nisab. Zakat is payable on accumulated wealth, especially gold and silver, merchandise, certain crops, certain livestock, and on subterranean and mineral wealth. As soon as it is collected it is redistributed to those in need, as defined in the Qur'an and the hadith. Zakat is one of the indispensable pillars of Islam.

**zakat al-fitr:** a small obligatory head-tax imposed on every responsible Muslim who has the means for himself and his dependants. It is paid once yearly at the end of

Ramadan just before the 'Id al-Fitr, the festival that marks the end of Ramadan

www.ingramcontent.com/pod-product-compliance
Lightning Source LLC
LaVergne TN
LVHW010356070526
838199LV00065B/5845